THE OFFICIAL

ENGLAND

SUPPORTERS' BOOK

THIS IS A CARLTON BOOK

This edition published in 1998

10 9 8 7 6 5 4 3 2 1

Text and design copyright © Carlton Books Limited 1998

The F.A. Crest is a registered trademark of The Football Association Limited

A CIP catalogue record for this book is available from the British Library

ISBN   1 85868 498 6 (hardback)
       1 85868 561 3 (paperback)

Project editors: Martin Corteel & Roland Hall
Project art direction: Diane Spender
Design assistant: Adam Wright
Production: Alexia Turner
Picture research: Justin Downing
Design: Nigel Davies

Printed in Italy

THE OFFICIAL
ENGLAND

SUPPORTERS' BOOK

DAVID COTTRELL

CARLTON

Contents

Glenn Hoddle: a new breed of England coach.

England fans in happy mood during qualifiers.

Introduction 7

Chapter 1
The Route to France 8

Relives England's qualifying campaign,

featuring reports from all eight ties and

comment from the men who mattered.

Chapter 2
Prospects for France 28

A look at England's opponents in the first

round and an analysis of the obstacles that

Hoddle's heroes must overcome.

Chapter 3
England's Star Players 36

Profiles of the players set to feature in the

squad, including career details, contribution to

the qualifiers and likely impact in the finals.

Chapter 4
The Coach 58

Recalls Hoddle's career as a player and

celebrates his success as national-team coach.

Chapter 5

World Cup History 66

Traces England's progress in the World Cup

from their first appearance in 1950 to their

heroic performance in 1990.

Chapter 6

Stars of the Past 90

From Bobby Charlton to Kevin Keegan to

Gary Lineker – a tribute to England's greatest

players over the last 40 years.

Chapter 7

World Cup Records 104

The complete statistical breakdown

of England in the World Cup – the

tournaments, the results and the goalscorers.

Index 110

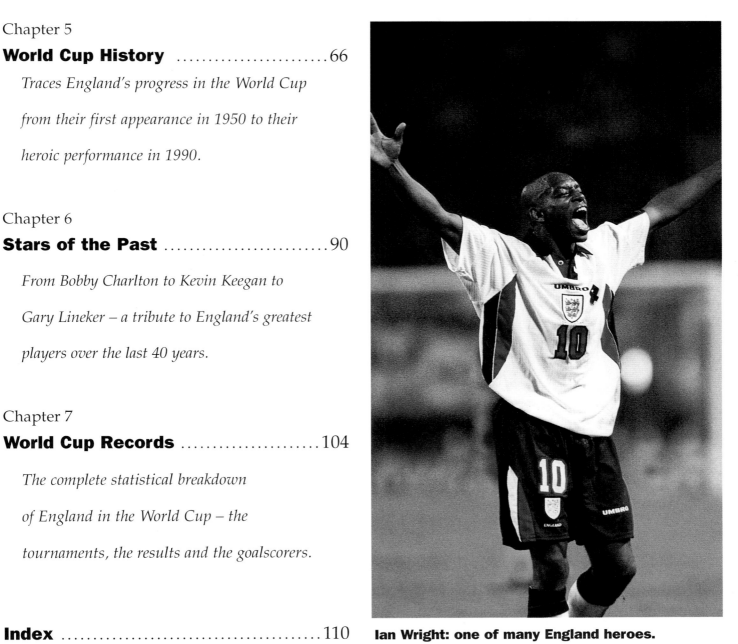

Ian Wright: one of many England heroes.

Introduction

Glenn Hoddle couldn't have put it better. When the final whistle blew in Rome last October, and England knew they had qualified for the World Cup in France, he simply shouted, "Get in there!"

After eight years in the wilderness, England are back where they belong – in the finals of the greatest sporting spectacle on the planet. This summer, they will compete with 31 other countries for the ultimate prize: a famous, glittering trophy and the title of world champions.

This guide contains all you need to know about England's romance with the World Cup and their prospects in the forthcoming tournament. There is a blow-by-blow account of their qualifying campaign, in-depth reports on the players upon whose shoulders rest the hopes and dreams of the nation, plus a profile of Glenn Hoddle, an account of life as a coach and a look back at former England managers who have guided their teams into the finals. There is also a history of England in past World Cups, featuring classic matches and tributes to the people's champions, followed by profiles of legendary England stars and the complete record of the three lions in the World Cup.

Illustrated throughout with classic pictures from past and present, this is every England fan's indispensable guide to the 1998 finals. On July 12, let's hope that those immortal words are uttered from the commentary box once again…

"It's only ten inches tall, it's solid gold – and it means that England have won the World Cup."

Graeme Le Saux celebrates a night of high drama and huge satisfaction in Rome.

Chapter 1
The Route to France

It was the summer of 1996, and England were on a high. They had lost to Germany, their old rivals, on penalties in the semi-finals of the European Championships, and great expectations had been heaped upon Glenn Hoddle, the new man in charge. At 38, and with 53 caps to his name, he was the youngest-ever England boss. But he was actually appointed while Terry Venables was still in charge.

After months of speculation, a press conference at Lancaster Gate on May 2 announced that Venables was stepping down after Euro 96 and Hoddle would be his successor. The former Chelsea manager, who signed a four-year contract commencing on June 1, was almost alone in wanting the hardest job in English football, but it seemed a natural progression. In footballing terms, they were two like-minded men. Both were close to their players but still commanded respect.

"If Terry had been manager when I was playing," declared Hoddle, "I think I would have won a lot more caps."

As the coach-in-waiting, Hoddle watched England progress to the last four of the tournament, playing some of their best football for years, sweeping along the entire nation on a tidal wave of emotion, restoring their pride and storming up the FIFA world-ranking table in the process. During his 28 months in charge of the national team, Venables had presided over 23 matches and England's record was: won 11, drawn 11, lost 1. Hoddle's brief was simple: follow that!

He inherited an upbeat squad, optimistic public and excitable media, plus a word of advice from his predecessor: "As England coach, you've got to know what you want to do tactically… Then you've got to sort out the players you want."

Hoddle wasn't exactly starting from scratch, but he was certainly facing new challenges. Prior to the European Championships, England hadn't played in a competitive match for over two years, and Venables had never led his team into battle abroad.

The draw for the 1998 World Cup qualifying groups pitched England against two new Eastern European republics, Georgia and Moldova, old adversaries, Poland, and the 1994 World Cup finalists, Italy. Only one country would qualify automatically for the finals in France, with eight runners-up throughout the European qualifying groups facing the lottery of a play-off.

For Hoddle and England, it was a formidable task. Both the Poles (1974) and the Italians (1978) had deprived England of a place in the World Cup finals back in the 1970s, while the Georgians and Moldovans, who could boast world-class players from the former Soviet Union, were an unknown quantity.

Say cheese! Glenn Hoddle's new England – coaching staff as well as players – line up for the cameras.

Qualification was imperative – the alternative was too bleak to contemplate. England had not reached the 1994 World Cup finals in the USA. If they failed again under Hoddle, over a decade would pass without an England team present at the greatest show on earth. In front of them lay 13 months of blood, sweat and tears, and it all began one hazy September afternoon near the shores of the Black Sea…

Moldova vs. England
Winning start

Where on earth was Chisinau? More than a few atlases were consulted in the summer of 1996 as England prepared for the first of eight World Cup qualifiers – a journey into the unknown against Moldova. A little research revealed that it was a former Soviet republic sandwiched between Romania and the Ukraine near the Black Sea, and Chisinau was the capital.

Moldova played their home games at the city's Republican Stadium. They had beaten Wales there in the not-too-distant past. This was England's first com-petitive match on foreign soil for the best part of three years, and it was Hoddle's first game in charge.

There were a number of withdrawals from the England squad through injury, and the new coach eventually settled on a side with just two new faces – Everton full-back Andy Hinchcliffe and Manchester United midfielder David Beckham. Just three weeks earlier, the precocious 21-year-old had scored a goal from the halfway line against Wimbledon. In the pre-match press conference in Chisinau, Hoddle confirmed that Beckham was ready for his international debut.

"This is the first time I'm going to work with the boy, and certain things might become apparent," he said. "Alex Ferguson knows him better than I do. What I will say is that with the ball at his feet, the lad can use it. Now we've got to find out if he's got the temperament. Has he got the character to go out and perform at the highest level?"

There was talk, too, about Hoddle's plan to create a club atmosphere among his squad. "Terry Venables was working towards it," he explained. "But to be fair, he only had two years in the job. I've got four, so I can plan a bit more long-term. It's important that all inter-national players, at whatever level, should be playing

Paul Gascoigne puts his bleach-blond head to good use in the win over Moldova.

within the same shape, philosophy and disciplines. The England way should be drummed into them. Then, of course, they'll go back to their clubs and play differently, but we're getting progress there, too."

For England's first tentative step on the road to France, the captain's armband was given to Alan Shearer, who became the country's 100th skipper in the process. He was a natural and popular choice. During the 1996 European Championships his goals had cemented his reputation as a formidable centre-forward with world-class credentials. When the team was announced, it featured three centre-halves, two wing-backs, three midfielders and two strikers. The sweeper system had arrived.

Some journalists expressed their doubts. Terry Venables, they insisted, had shied away from the formation, claiming that the use of wing-backs was too defensive. Instead, Venables had deployed attacking midfielders or even strikers in wide positions.

But Hoddle stuck to his guns. "Don't judge this team as the image of what I'm building long-term," he warned. "First and foremost, we've got to get three points. If I don't get the results, I don't have a long term. I'm the one with my head on the chopping block."

Two-goal burst

He need not have worried. Despite one or two early scares, his team cruised past Moldova with goals from Nick Barmby, Paul Gascoigne and Alan Shearer. The first came after 24 minutes, and it was a direct result of attacking wing-back play.

Hinchcliffe overhit a cross from the left, but it was retrieved by Gary Neville, whose fast, low ball was dispatched on the half-volley by Barmby. It was the Middlesbrough striker's third goal in five starts.

A minute later, it was two. Paul Ince broke up a Moldovan attack, passed to Barmby. Ince hooked the return ball over to Gascoigne, who headed bravely over goalkeeper Denis Romanenco.

Five minutes before the interval, Shearer was denied a clear penalty when he was hauled down in the box. Seconds later, he blazed wide with the goal at his mercy. But in the second half he made amends, scoring his 11th goal in 29 internationals by clipping the ball over Romanenco after good work from Neville and Gareth Southgate.

There was just time for Matthew Le Tissier to make a late entry as a substitute for Barmby and Moldova's

Testimitanu to crash a penalty-kick against the crossbar before Finnish referee Ilca Koho blew the final whistle.

The only blot on England's performance was two needless yellow cards, picked up by Stuart Pearce and man of the match Paul Ince. But the plus points were many. The new caps had settled in well, the 3–5–2 formation had come through unscathed, and Hoddle's England was beginning to take shape.

"Ten years ago," said the coach, "if someone had said that we were going to play with a flat back-three, the players would have been up in arms. But times are changing. It's going to be a slow evolution."

The result was greeted with cautious enthusiasm by the Press. The following Monday, *The Daily Telegraph* proclaimed, "Three goals, three points and three lions back in business."

Alan Shearer gets stuck into the Moldovans.

SEPTEMBER 1, 1996, CHISINAU

Moldova 0
England 3 (Barmby 24, Gascoigne 25, Shearer 61)
Att: 9,500

Moldova: Romanenco, Secu, Nani, Testimitanu, Gaidamasciuc, Belous (Siscin 58), Epureanu, Curtianu, Clescenco, Miterev (Rebeja 61), Popovici.

England: Seaman, G. Neville, Pearce, Southgate, Pallister, Hinchcliffe, Ince, Gascoigne (Batty 81), Beckham, Shearer, Barmby (Le Tissier 81).

Group Two table

	P	W	D	L	F	A	Pts
England	1	1	0	0	3	0	3
Georgia	0	0	0	0	0	0	0
Italy	0	0	0	0	0	0	0
Poland	0	0	0	0	0	0	0
Moldova	1	0	0	1	0	3	0

England vs. Poland
Unconvincing victory

Hoddle's Wembley debut as England coach was against Poland, those old adversaries, and all the signs pointed towards a comfortable home win. The Poles hadn't won in their previous 12 matches and had only recently recalled Antoni Piechniczek as coach. But Piechniczek was a wily old warrior who had guided his country to the World Cup finals in 1982 and 1986, and in 32-year-old playmaker Piotr Nowak, they had a dangerous and experienced schemer in midfield.

Prior to the game, the Press concentrated upon Hoddle's new sweeper system and the comments he had made after the game in Moldova about England internationals learning to play the coach's way. At the press conference at Bisham Abbey, he was determined to set the record straight.

"I've never asked our clubs to play in the same way as the England team," he told the assembled journalists. "I think what I said was misinterpreted. I would never, ever expect club managers to play in a way that suited international football.

"I said that I wanted to play a certain way, but I also knew I was not going to be able to play in exactly the way I wanted because I'm not working with these players every day. It's too much to cram it all into six or seven days. When I say how I want my team to play, there's certain patterns and balances that I'll keep whatever the shape is. The shape might change, but the balance will still be there."

Sure enough, Hoddle altered the personnel in a virtually unchanged formation. He fielded three at the back in Gary Neville, Gareth Southgate and Stuart Pearce. A four-man midfield featured Paul Gascoigne and Paul Ince, with David Beckham and Andy Hinchcliffe pushing wide. Up front, Steve McManaman was instructed to operate behind the formidable Newcastle duo, Alan Shearer and Les Ferdinand.

England's early shock

Poland, however, were in no mood to play second fiddle. With Nowak providing a dynamic link between defence and attack, they dominated the early exchanges and opened the scoring on seven minutes when Marek Citko nipped in behind Gary Neville to

Les Ferdinand soars high against the Poles – as England make it two out of two.

caught the eye. By general consent, the Manchester United midfielder had adjusted to the demands of international football and was growing in stature.

Overall, however, Hoddle accepted that it had not been an attractive match. The centre-circle had been congested throughout the 90 minutes and at times the service to the strikers left a lot to be desired.

"The game was too open for my liking," he admitted. "We were trying to go through the eye of a needle in midfield instead of working the wide defenders, and we were not defending correctly in front of the back-three. I knew Poland would defend deep, and in numbers, and it was always going to be difficult to get to the bye-line because of the way Poland play. Their pushed-in full-backs were doing a defensive job, and that's why I had Hinchcliffe and Beckham wide, because they don't have to go past people to get decent crosses in. They've got the ability to bend balls in. They did it at times, but the delivery could have been better."

England's second consecutive victory in the qualifiers had kept them on top of their group. Italy were second, but encouragingly they had laboured hard to beat Georgia on the same evening.

For all that, there was no shortage of post-match criticism. The English Press – predictably – wanted more. *The Sunday Times* dubbed it an "unconvincing victory," while *The Observer* mused, "An opinion already forming is that England might struggle on the road to France were Shearer ever to be indisposed for

intercept a cross from the right and fire past David Seaman from close range. To their credit, England refused to panic and as the half wore on, the flat back-three found its feet and Shearer began to make his presence felt up front.

The equalizer came on 24 minutes when Polish goalkeeper Andrzej Wozniak missed a cross from Beckham and Shearer headed into an empty net to calm the home side's nerves. Fourteen minutes later, England were ahead, Ferdinand diverting a cross into the path of Shearer, who lashed home an unstoppable shot from the edge of the box. It was superb finishing from a striker who was rapidly establishing himself as one of the deadliest marksmen in the business.

Despite one or two scares – Seaman saved superbly from Nowak two minutes before the interval – England remained in control and could have increased their lead through Ferdinand twice in the last five minutes. In a close and often frustrating game, another tidy performance from David Beckham

---

OCTOBER 9, 1996, WEMBLEY

England 2 (Shearer 24, 38)
Poland 1 (Citko 7)
Att: 74,663

England: Seaman, G. Neville, Pearce, Southgate (Pallister 51), Hinchcliffe, McManaman, Ince, Gascoigne, Beckham, Shearer, Ferdinand.

Poland: Wozniak, Waldoch, Zielinski, Juskowiak, Hajto, Michalski, Baluszynski, Wojtala, Nowak, Citko, Warzycha (Sagamowski 75).

Other results
Moldova 1, Italy 3 (5/9/96)
Italy 1, Georgia 0 (9/10/96)

Group Two table

	P	W	D	L	F	A	Pts
England	2	2	0	0	5	1	6
Italy	2	2	0	0	4	1	6
Georgia	1	0	0	1	0	1	0
Poland	1	0	0	1	1	2	0
Moldova	2	0	0	2	1	6	0

Another typically combative performance by Alan Shearer earned him two goals against Poland.

any length of time."

In time, the newspaper's fears were to be realised, but history would tell a very different story.

Georgia vs. England
Another good away win

So to Georgia a month later, and another trip into unknown territory. Located on the southern borders of Russia in the shadow of the Caucasus, the newly-independent state had a proud footballing past. Dynamo Tbilisi, the old army club, had been a force in Soviet and European football, and on paper at least, the national team were a tougher proposition than Moldova, even though they had won only once in their six previous internationals.

Their skilful play revolved around Manchester City's mercurial midfielder, Georgiou Kinkladze, and after their 1–0 defeat in Italy four weeks earlier, their coach Alexander Chivadze had vowed, "We will beat England."

It was England's last match of the year, and Hoddle took great pleasure in welcoming Tony Adams back into the fold. Arsenal's towering centre-half was winning the battle against his drink problem, and the England coach had no hesitation in naming him in the starting line-up.

"I've been encouraged by Tony's performances playing in the centre of Arsenal's three defenders," he explained. "He wasn't fit enough to be included last time, but now he's lean and sharp, and he's defending excellently."

Less heartening was the absence of Alan Shearer with a groin injury and a domestic incident between Paul Gascoigne and his wife which had made headline news back home, with most newspaper journalists calling for the player's head. Hoddle, who delayed his team selection until he had spoken to Gascoigne on the day before the game, decided to stand by the wayward genius.

"What a great example Paul will be if he can change," he said. "What a challenge, to make him into a role model. I'm hoping that in two years' time we will look back and see this as a turning point. Paul has given football some fantastic moments, but he's also given football some headaches. We're trying to give him the aspirin to get rid of the headaches. If we can do that, I think he can get back to his very best, and possibly be even better, because at 29 he should be hitting his peak."

Hoddle accepted that Gascoigne may have lost his turn of pace. But he also argued that the Rangers midfielder could more than compensate for his apparent lack of stamina by using his head. "The experience he has now means that he won't need to use his legs so much because his mind will tell him what's going to happen next. He needs to find out what he can do and what he can't do, physically, and then adjust accordingly. I still think he's at his best in and around the opposing penalty area. If he can adjust to working there, he still has a lot to offer." However he played, Gascoigne knew that his every move would come under intense scrutiny. But pressure was nothing new to the midfield ace.

A welcome return to England duty for Arsenal's inspirational defender, Tony Adams.

David Beckham, Manchester United's gifted young midfielder, had an impressive game in Tbilisi.

Sheringham shines

With Shearer missing, it was also a chance for Teddy Sheringham to regain his place in the side. On a sunny winter's day in Georgia's capital, the Tottenham striker had a magnificent match, scoring England's first goal – his fifth in 21 appearances – and providing a delightful assist for their second.

A quarter of an hour into the game, he latched on to Ferdinand's through-ball and finished clinically with the outside of his right boot. Just over 20 minutes later, he returned the compliment, receiving the ball after a trademark Gascoigne dribble and playing it into Ferdinand's path. The powerful Newcastle striker shrugged off his marker with ease to fire home.

In truth, the 2–0 scoreline flattered the Georgians. Apart from an early flourish from a few of their technically-gifted individuals, they were no match for a powerful England team who subdued the partisan crowd and played some delightful possession football on an awkward, bumpy pitch.

After the game, Hoddle singled out David Batty, his midfield enforcer, and Sol Campbell, who made his first start in a three-man central defence, for praise. Captain Tony Adams, who has been in and out of the England squad, was a giant at the back.

Hoddle had continued his 100 per cent start in international management. In scoring terms, England had gone one better than nearest Group Two rivals Italy, who had inexplicably found the Georgians a tough nut to crack at home. "We've now got a psychological advantage when we play Italy in February," claimed the coach. "So I can go and have a good Christmas!"

It was also a time for Hoddle to assess his team's progress so far. "We learned a lot from our game against Poland at Wembley," he added. "Everyone went out and played like individuals that night and normally if you play like that at international level, you're lucky to get a draw. But we got three points despite the performance, which was a good sign. Against Georgia we played as a team, and you could see the difference."

NOVEMBER 9, 1996, TBILISI

Georgia 0
England 2 (Sheringham 15, Ferdinand 37)
Att: 48,000

Georgia: Zoidze, Lobjanidze, Tskhadadze, Shelia, Georgiashvili (Gudushauri 60), Nemsadze, Kinkladze, Jamarauli, Kobiashvili, Ketsbaia, S. Arveladze (Gogrichiani 52).

England: Seaman, Campbell, Hinchcliffe, Southgate, Adams, Batty, Ince, Gascoigne, Beckham, Sheringham, Ferdinand (Wright 81).

Group Two table

	P	W	D	L	F	A	Pts
England	3	3	0	0	7	1	9
Italy	2	2	0	0	4	1	6
Poland	1	0	0	1	1	2	0
Georgia	2	0	0	2	0	3	0
Moldova	2	0	0	2	1	6	0

Alan Shearer is shackled by Italy's Fabio Cannavaro in a frustrating night at Wembley.

England vs. Italy
Another Roman conquest

Three months passed before England's next qualifier – the eagerly awaited clash with Italy at Wembley. When it finally arrived, it was instantly forgettable. It rained – how it rained – on a night when Glenn Hoddle's best-laid plans were disrupted by a rash of injuries and a smash-and-grab raid by the Italians.

Hoddle went into the match without David Seaman, Tony Adams, Paul Gascoigne and Teddy Sheringham, and there were doubts over the fitness of Paul Ince and Alan Shearer. The absence of Gascoigne, in particular, was a tremendous blow.

"He might have been able to influence the game more coming on as a substitute, rather than starting," said the England coach before the game. "But all that went out of the window because of his injury."

Circumstances beyond his control forced Hoddle to rethink both his team selection and his tactics. Denied the services of the hugely influential David Seaman, he named Ian Walker as goalkeeper. Stuart Pearce, an orthodox left-back, would play at centre-half alongside Sol Campbell, with Gary Neville and Graeme Le Saux occupying the full-back berths. David Batty, Paul Ince, David Beckham and Steve McManaman were to patrol midfield. Shearer, struggling for full fitness, would partner Matthew Le Tissier up front.

Italy, on the other hand, had a wealth of options. Coach Cesare Maldini had been charged with restoring the side's confidence and flair after their dismal showing at Euro 96, and a victory at Wembley would lay any lingering demons to rest. "I have been looking forward to this game with England for a long time," revealed Maldini. "It should be a classic match."

As it was, Hoddle's programme notes proved to be painfully prophetic. "Italy have great talent and discipline," he wrote. "In many ways, having a new manager in Cesare Maldini might work in their favour because they were feeling the pressure somewhat under their previous coach Arrigo Sacchi. They have some highly talented players and I'm sure England fans will be watching Gianfranco Zola closely."

Zola takes his chance

It took Chelsea's pocket dynamo just 18 minutes to plunge his adopted country into despair. Running on to a slide-rule pass from defender Alessandro Costacurta, he beat Ian Walker at his near post with a vicious shot. Only 60 seconds earlier, Matthew Le Tissier – a controversial choice in attack – had spurned a golden opportunity to put England ahead by taking a split-second too long to control a cross from Stuart Pearce.

When Zola scored, the best part of 75,000 spectators sat and stared in silence. Over the 90 minutes, England had 12 shots to Italy's two. But try as they might, they couldn't find the net. Indeed, they were not so much robbed as mugged by Italy's stealth and cunning. It was their first World Cup defeat at Wembley. The Italians were now level on points in the

group with a game in hand. It was Hoddle's first defeat as England coach, but he remained defiant, describing it as a set-back rather than a disaster and calling for some perspective.

"We are not out of the World Cup yet," he declared. "By no means are we out of this competition. There is a lot of football to be played. I don't think on that performance I can say that they were technically better than us. They were on the back foot and might have wobbled had we got an early goal. It was always going to be a case of limited chances at both ends, and we limited them more then they limited us."

Nonetheless, criticism from certain quarters was inevitable. After England's intoxicating start to their qualifying campaign, the defeat by Italy felt like an almighty hangover, and there was a predictable tide of self-doubt instigated by the press. One journalist wrote that, "England's cloak and dagger preparation, as well as their performance, suffered by comparison with the cool professionalism of the Italians," while another described the match as "A familiar tale of Anglo-Saxon broadsword against a stiletto." A third lamented, "If only England could be so dull and negative in Rome come October".

By contrast, the Italian newspapers were full of euphoria, bombast and a renewed self-belief. One of the country's leading journals, *Gazzetta dello Sport*, proclaimed, "It was the last big party the legendary Wembley will see. The era of the Empire Stadium will

David Batty beats Roberto di Matteo to the ball as England go down fighting.

FEBRUARY 12, 1997, WEMBLEY

England 0
Italy 1 (Zola 18)
Att: 75,055

England: Walker, G. Neville, Pearce, Campbell, Le Saux, Batty (Wright 88), Ince, Beckham, McManaman (Merson 79), Le Tissier (Ferdinand 60), Shearer.

Italy: Peruzzi, Ferrara, Costacurta, Cannavaro, Di Livio, D. Baggio, Albertini, Di Matteo, Maldini, Zola (Fuser 90), Casiraghi (Ravanelli 76).

Other result:
Poland 2, Moldova 1 (10/11/96)

Group Two table

	P	W	D	L	F	A	Pts
England	4	3	0	1	7	2	9
Italy	3	3	0	0	5	1	9
Poland	2	1	0	1	3	3	3
Georgia	2	0	0	2	0	3	0
Moldova	3	0	0	3	2	8	0

never again see a team like Italy before it is demolished. Never again will it witness a game as important as this. It didn't matter that the stadium was dressed in the red and white cross of St George. It didn't matter that the tempest of rain was choreographed. Over the years it must have seemed to the opposition teams that have played there that the god of the skies was English. He wasn't on Wednesday."

England vs. Georgia
England back on track

A 2–0 victory over Mexico in a friendly at the end of March provided a minor distraction from the World Cup, but England still had 10 weeks to mull over the defeat by Italy.

A return to form at Wembley against the Georgians was imperative, not just for qualification but for morale. In front of another full house, they got the win they so desperately needed – a repeat of their victory in Tbilisi back in November 1996.

Georgia arrived with a new coach, David Kipiani, and the dual threat of Georgiou Kinkladze and Newcastle-bound Temur Ketsbaia. But again, they were overwhelmed by a physically superior England side which dominated proceedings from start to finish.

Before the match, England's Italian-based midfielder Paul Ince had made a point of talking up the English game. "There is so much said about the foreign players and their technique that our lads can be a bit in awe of them," he revealed. "But playing against them every week has taught me not to worry.

"The Italians, though, are more clever about attacking. They play it perfectly. They know when to go for it and when not. They'll hang back and wait for their chance, like they did against us at Wembley. They got a goal then defended for their lives. We've got to think a bit more about how we're going to play."

Ince was emerging as an increasingly important member of the England team, and Hoddle was aware of the player's improvement at Internazionale: "Paul has gained experience and added to his talent in going abroad and taking on that challenge."

Shearer and Sheringham reunited

Ince played at the heart of a midfield which included David Batty, Robert Lee and David Beckham. Injury prevented Paul Gascoigne from making his 49th appearance for his country. In defence, Stuart Pearce made way for the fit-again Tony Adams, while Gary Neville, Graeme Le Saux and the ever-maturing Sol Campbell kept their places. But the most exciting development was up front, where Alan Shearer and Teddy Sheringham were together for the first time in

(left) Pick that one out! Alan Shearer crashes England's second goal past Georgia's forlorn wall and goalkeeper.

(right) In a morale-boosting win over Georgia, Shearer displayed all the qualities that have made him a top-class striker.

a competitive match since Euro 96.

It took England until the final two minutes of the first half to break down the Georgians, whose marking was tighter than in the first encounter between the two teams. After Lee had hit the post with a beautifully-flighted chip, Le Saux found Shearer in space on the left. The England skipper killed the ball with his chest, waited for Sheringham to make his run across goal and found his head with a perfectly-weighted pass.

In the second half, Kinkladze showed some nice touches and received warm applause when he was substituted after 60 minutes. With his departure went any Georgian hopes of an equalizer. A quarter of an hour from the end, there was a minor scare when his team-mate Tskhadadze shaved Seaman's crossbar with a speculative shot, but the effort merely galvanized England into action.

With the 90 minutes all but up, Georgian goalkeeper Zoidze handled a back-pass and England were awarded an indirect free-kick in the penalty area. Sheringham back-heeled the ball to Shearer, who almost burst the net with a ferocious shot. Mission accomplished, and team selection justified.

"I wanted Teddy to drop back and link the play, so I needed a bit of threat from midfield off the ball," explained Hoddle, who gave his side a modest 7 out of 10 for a performance blighted only by bookings for Ince, Beckham and Le Saux. "Robert Lee is in good form. He loves to get in the box off the ball, and I felt that was the type of support that Alan Shearer needed."

In the press conference after the match, Hoddle learned that Italy had won 3–0 at home to preserve their four-point lead at the top of the group, albeit having played a game more. With England's all-important trip to Poland looming, the topic of conversation turned to Paul Gascoigne, that most glaring of absentees.

"I don't think Paul will ever get back to what he was five years ago because of his injuries," conceded the England coach. "But he can get close. I've spoken to him at length and now it's up to him, not me.

"Of course there's a chance of him playing in Poland. First of all, he's got to show me that he's in good shape, fitness-wise, then he's got to be playing well. And longer term, there are things wrong in his life that he's got to address. It is up to him. He's still within the period of time I'm prepared to give him, and I'm saying, 'Can you learn?'. If he can't, there's another side to me that will come out if it needs to."

The message from Hoddle was clear, but was Gazza ready to respond?

APRIL 30, 1997, WEMBLEY

England 2 (Sheringham 43, Shearer 90)
Georgia 0
Att: 71,208

England: Seaman, G. Neville, Le Saux, Campbell, Adams (Southgate 87), Batty, Ince (Redknapp 78), Lee, Beckham, Sheringham, Shearer.

Georgia: Zoidze, Chikhradze, Sheqiladze, Tskhadadze, Shelia, Machavariani (Gogrichiani 30, A. Arveladze 76), Nemsadze, Jamarauli, Ketsbaia, Kinkladze (Gakhokidze 61), S. Arveladze.

Other results:
Italy 3, Moldova 0 (29/3/97)
Poland 0, Italy 0 (2/4/97)
Italy 3 Poland 0 (30/4/97)

Group Two table

	P	W	D	L	F	A	Pts
Italy	6	5	1	0	11	1	16
England	5	4	0	1	9	2	12
Poland	4	1	1	2	3	6	4
Georgia	3	0	0	3	0	5	0
Moldova	4	0	0	4	2	11	0

Poland vs. England
Top-two finish guaranteed

At the end of May, the England squad touched down in Poland, where they had not won since 1966. Eight weeks earlier, Italy had been held to a goalless draw by the Poles in Katowice. An England win would close the gap on Italy to one point, with both countries having played six games.

The previous Saturday, England had beaten South Africa 2–1 in a friendly at Old Trafford. Hoddle, of course, had taken few risks, resting eight members of the team who had beaten Georgia at Wembley. One notable exception, however, was Robert Lee, who topped a fine display in Manchester with a goal and retained the midfield grafter's role ahead of David Batty for the Poland game. Paul Gascoigne, who had been stretchered off at Old Trafford after a crude challenge in stoppage time, was passed fit to play.

Prior to the match, Hoddle complained to FIFA about the state of the pitch in Chorzow, in particular the height of the grass. He needn't have worried. From the kick-off, England mastered the slippery surface –

Paul Ince played arguably his finest game for England in the crucial win in Poland – but a yellow card ruined his evening and kept him out of the next match against Moldova.

and their opponents – to run out 2–0 winners. For the second consecutive qualifier, Shearer and Sheringham got the goals. The only downside was another booking for Ince. It was his second yellow card and it meant that he would miss the next match.

After the debate about his fitness and attitude, Gascoigne limped out with a badly-cut thigh just 17 minutes into the game. He was replaced by David Batty, who supported Lee and Paul Ince in midfield.

Southgate's triumphant return

Alongside Gary Neville and Sol Campbell in defence, there was a welcome return for Gareth Southgate in place of the injured Tony Adams. The Aston Villa centre-half had been omitted from the side which lost to Italy and by his own admission had suffered a crisis of confidence. Against Poland, he was a rock. Down the flanks, Graeme Le Saux and David Beckham worked tirelessly.

England's opener was textbook stuff. After five minutes, Ince won a loose ball in the sodden centre-circle and drove forward. As the red-stockinged legs closed in, he split the Polish defence with an inch-perfect pass to Shearer, who homed in from the right and met the ball first time, crashing it with training-ground arrogance and precision beyond the dive of goalkeeper

Andrzej Wozniak and into the bottom corner of the net.

It was a hugely satisfying goal, as Gareth Southgate later revealed: "Before we went to Poland, Glenn Hoddle arranged a number of training sessions where we would play a keep-ball game. He was encouraging us to look forward early, and you can see that it worked a treat against Poland. The longer you allow international opponents to regroup behind the ball, the less chance you have of scoring."

Five minutes after Shearer's goal, England looked to have conceded a penalty when Beckham brought down the dangerous Majak in the penalty area. But the Swiss referee awarded an indirect free-kick to England for an earlier offside. To compound Poland's misery, England won their own spot-kick three minutes into injury time at the end of the first half when Shearer was held down. Amazingly, the Newcastle striker's low shot struck the base of the left-hand post and rebounded to safety.

The miss gave the home side renewed hope going into the interval. But England refused to sit back on their slender lead and in the final minute of the match they put the result beyond doubt. Lee sprang the offside trap, rounded the goalkeeper to set up an easy chance for Sheringham, and the points belonged to England. It was just reward for their positive approach to the match.

"I hope that this is the game that will make people look forward," said Hoddle. "This team has never had

Shearer magic! Another goal for the England ace.

England vs. Moldova
England in the driving seat

Something fabulous happened to England over the remainder of the summer. Hard on the heels of the win in Poland, they beat Italy and France, narrowly lost to Brazil, but won the respect and admiration of the world as well as Le Tournoi. The French tournament was an unqualified success – the culmination of 11 dizzy days which saw the national team rise up the FIFA rankings list and, most importantly, realize Glenn Hoddle's dream of versatile, adventurous football.

Assistant coach John Gorman summed it up thus, "We played against three of the top sides in the business and came away having won the tournament."

It had also given Hoddle the chance to refine his 3–5–2 system and look at one or two new faces. Prior to the tournament, he had insisted, "We are going there to be professional. If we want to win the World Cup, we are going to have to make sacrifices."

After the hard slog of the domestic season, his players responded magnificently. ITV commentator Brian Moore, who followed England's progress closely, remarked, "We all know about Glenn Hoddle's skills and tactical acumen, but the way he has stamped a code of behaviour and discipline on the camp reminds me of Sir Alf Ramsey. Travelling around with the squad, you notice how incredibly focused the players are."

With the emergence of new stars like Paul Scholes,

to come to places like this to get a result. We had to be on the front foot, we had to be thinking of victory."

The win in Chorzow set the tone for what was to be an exciting summer. No sooner had the final whistle been blown than England were preparing for a mini-tournament in France featuring the World Cup hosts, plus Italy and Brazil.

"I don't mind what happens in France now," added Hoddle. "But if we had lost here and won Le Tournoi, it wouldn't have been a happy summer for me."

Once more, England were dreaming of automatic qualification. Their penultimate match in Group Two was at home to Moldova – a walkover on paper – while the Italians had a difficult journey to Georgia. After that, England and Italy would meet in Rome in what was already being billed as the big decider. The tension was beginning to mount.

MAY 31, 1997, CHORZOW

Poland 0
England 2 (Shearer 6, Sheringham 90)
Att: 35,000

Poland: Wozniak, Jozwiak, Zielinski, Kaluzny, Ledwon, Bukalski (P. Swierczewski 46), Nowak (Kucharski 57), Majak, Waldoch, Juskowiak (Adamczyk 51), Dembinski.

England: Seaman, G. Neville, Le Saux, Campbell, Southgate, Ince, Lee, Gascoigne (Batty 17), Beckham (P. Neville 88), Sheringham, Shearer.

Group Two table

	P	W	D	L	F	A	Pts
Italy	6	5	1	0	11	1	16
England	6	5	0	1	11	2	15
Poland	5	1	1	3	8	4	4
Georgia	3	0	0	3	0	5	0
Moldova	4	0	0	4	2	11	0

Paul Scholes, a revelation over the summer, took his chance against Moldova.

Catch me if you can! Ian Wright celebrates his second goal – and England's fourth – against Moldova.

who scored in the 2–0 win over Italy in Montpellier, there was a healthy competition for places and a bubbly atmosphere within the camp. The victory against Italy, in particular, was an enormous psychological boost.

"This is an England team trying to play football the way their coach played," claimed French footballing legend Michel Platini. Everyone, it seemed, was mightily impressed.

Twelve months after his first game in charge, it was also a time for Hoddle to reflect. "I've told the players that in club terms, we've done our pre-season work, but we're only three or four games into the league programme," said the coach. "But I think we're learning as a team, and with new faces coming in, I feel it is my England, if you like."

Shearer's shocking injury

Hoddle was keen to keep the momentum going for the visit of Moldova in September. A month before the match, however, he received the news that Alan Shearer had ruptured his ankle ligaments in a pre-season friendly at Goodison Park and would be out until the New Year. It was a major blow, but worse was to follow.

The death of Diana, Princess of Wales cast a shadow over the whole country, and it would be an emotional and difficult night at Wembley. England had to be professional. A win would put them on top of Group Two for the first time in seven months.

Earlier in the evening, Italy had managed only a goalless draw in Georgia, and *Gazzetta dello Sport* was losing patience. "Someone should have told Cesare Maldini that a draw in Tbilisi was not a useful, old-fashioned away point but was just the same as losing," it groaned.

Moldova, still without a point after five games, looked easy meat. But they had pride to play for, and they would be difficult to break down. Expecting them to defend in depth, Hoddle searched for width. In England's pre-match training sessions, he put his squad through "wave" drills: seven players would attack another seven in quick succession.

He explained, "At this level, a lot of teams get behind the ball in numbers, and we're looking for the movement to open them up."

With this in mind, he chose a mobile, attack-minded team. Graeme Le Saux had broken his elbow playing for Chelsea, so Hoddle drafted in Phil Neville, one of the stars of Le Tournoi, as a wing-back, with David Beckham on the opposite flank. The back-three – Southgate, Campbell and Gary Neville – remained unchanged. In midfield, David Batty would operate behind Paul Gascoigne and Paul Scholes, another revelation over the summer.

Up front, there were enforced changes. Shearer's partner in crime, Teddy Sheringham, was out with two cracked ribs. But England were nothing if not spoilt for strikers. Ian Wright, who had scored against the Italians at Le Tournoi but lost his place against Poland, returned to partner Les Ferdinand, whose last cap was against Italy at Wembley.

In the end, it was easy. The increasingly impressive Scholes found the net with a diving header from a Beckham cross. Paul Gascoigne set up Ian Wright for number two at the start of the second half.

After 81 minutes, Gascoigne scored a marvellous solo goal, and Wright rounded it off with a clinical finish at the death for his second. Next stop, Rome, and a date with destiny.

SEPTEMBER 10, 1997, WEMBLEY

England 4 (Scholes 28, Wright 46, 90, Gascoigne 81)
Moldova 0
Att: 74,102

England: Seaman, G. Neville, P. Neville, Campbell, Southgate, Batty, Gascoigne, Beckham (Ripley 68, Butt 76), Scholes, Ferdinand (Collymore 83), Wright.

Moldova: Romanenco, Fistikan, Testimitanu, Culibaba (Suharev 53), Spynu, Stroenco, Curtianu, Sischin (Popovici 61), Miterev, Rebeja, Rogachev (Cibotari 75).

Other results
Georgia 2, Moldova 0 (7/6/97)
Poland 4, Georgia 1 (14/6/97)
Georgia 0, Italy 0 (10/9/97)

Group Two table

	P	W	D	L	F	A	Pts
England	7	6	0	1	15	2	18
Italy	7	5	2	0	11	1	17
Poland	6	2	1	3	7	9	7
Georgia	6	1	1	4	3	9	4
Moldova	6	0	0	6	2	17	0

Italy vs. England
Mission accomplished!

"We've played more than three minutes of injury time, and I really don't know what this ref is doing!" Brian Moore's commentary, everyone else's thoughts. Italy 0, England 0. Fever pitch in the Stadio Olimpico. Time up on the clock. The final whistle about to go, surely…

It was always going to be a heart-stopper. The Italians had to win to qualify automatically. A draw would see England through. They hadn't won in Italy for 36 years. Since then, the two countries had met 11 times, with seven victories for Italy and three for England – in England, America and most recently at Le Tournoi in France. Ancient history, admittedly, but England knew they had the measure of their opponents.

This was Glenn Hoddle's 13th game in charge, 16 months after he replaced Terry Venables as coach and two weeks before his 40th birthday. At the pre-match press conference, he described it as "the biggest game I've been involved in as a manager. I feel very proud to be carrying the nation's hopes, and I know the players do, too. We've got the whole country behind us. It's just like Euro 96 all over again, and we've got our destiny in our own hands. I feel inspired, rather than a sense of burden."

Hoddle the coach became Hoddle the psychiatrist. "Focus" was the buzzword around England's headquarters. "If we're to get the right result," he continued, "I need to pay attention to what's going on in the players' minds, and in their stomachs. When they leave that

Teddy Sheringham keeps his cool during a tempestuous night in Rome.

Gareth Southgate capped a timely return to form with a sterling display against the Italians.

dressing-room, every single one of them has got to have that inner confidence that says, 'We're going to get this result.' If they have that belief, it'll see them through."

He was playing his cards close to his chest and indulging in a little kidology along the way. Gareth Southgate seemed to be carrying a thigh injury. David Beckham was having breathing difficulties in training. The Press – both English and Italian – fell for it hook, line and sinker. "Hoddle may seem calm," wrote the *Daily Mail's* correspondent, "but is paranoia beginning to take hold beneath the ice-cool surface?"

Southgate had a slight dead leg, Beckham a minor cold. Both laid it on thick. Hoddle's only real problem was tactical. Italy would probably fluctuate between 4–4–2 and 4–3–3, so he needed a strong defence and midfield. In the end, he sacrificed Gary Neville for the more experienced Tony Adams alongside Southgate and Sol Campbell in a flat back-three, with support from wing-backs Beckham, making his eighth consecutive appearance in the qualifiers, and Le Saux. In midfield, Sheringham would drop deep to help out Batty, Gascoigne and skipper Paul Ince. The lone striker was Ian Wright.

Game on

Enter the gladiators. After all the talk, all the speculation, it was time to settle Group Two. Italy surged forward on a tidal wave of emotion. England ran on adrenalin – and refused to give an inch. The hosts had most of the possession, but the visitors had the best chances. The first came on 29 minutes. An Ince volley from 18 yards was beaten away by goalkeeper Angelo Peruzzi. On the hour, Seaman saved superbly from Enrico Chiesa.

Italy began to panic. The coach's son, Paolo Maldini, went off, and Beckham found more room on the right. Campbell was booked for an innocuous challenge on Filippo Inzaghi. If England survived, he would miss the first game in France. But he kept his cool, even when Angelo di Livio crashed into him and received a red card.

Batty guarded the space in front of his defenders. Gascoigne dictated the flow of the game with his passing. Adams won everything in the air. Southgate made vital tackles. Le Saux held his ground. Sheringham ran and ran. And on 92 minutes, Wright,

England heroes Paul Ince and Paul Gascoigne show what it means to qualify for the World Cup finals.

who had held the ball up for his midfielders all night, rounded Peruzzi but flicked the ball against the post. Within seconds, a header from Christian Vieri flew inches wide of Seaman's right-hand upright. And finally, memorably, sensationally, Dutch referee Mario van der Ende blew his whistle.

Italy, who had won all of their previous 15 World Cup ties at Rome, were inconsolable. *Gazzetta dello Sport*, which had crowed so loudly eight months earlier, hailed a new force in world football: "Italy are inferior to England. They are not as assured in their play, they cannot match their control of a game, nor their adaptability. The lions who once knew only how to hoof the ball, tackle, cross and mix it, now dribble with skill, take control of the action, take possession with elegance and look for the winning chance."

There could be no higher praise. In the Eternal City, Hoddle's heroes had become immortal. Roll on 1998!

OCTOBER 11, 1997, ROME

Italy 0
England 0
Att: 81,200

Italy: Peruzzi, Nesta, Costacurta, Cannavaro, Di Livio, Albertini, D. Baggio, Maldini (Benarrivo 31), Zola (Del Piero 63), Vieri, Inzaghi (Chiesa 46).

England: Seaman, Campbell, Le Saux, Adams, Southgate, Batty, Ince, Gascoigne (Butt 89), Beckham, Sheringham, Wright.

Other results:
Moldova 0, Georgia 1 (24/9/97)
Moldova 0, Poland 3 (7/10/97)
Georgia 3, Poland 0 (11/10/97)

Group Two (final standings)

	P	W	D	L	F	A	Pts
England	8	6	1	1	15	2	19
Italy	8	5	3	0	11	1	18
Poland	8	3	1	4	10	12	10
Georgia	8	3	1	4	7	9	10
Moldova	8	0	0	8	2	21	0

England's 1998 World Cup qualifying campaign

ENGLAND'S RESULTS						
Date	Team	Venue	Result	Score	Scorers	Att.
1.9.96	Moldova	Chisinau	W	3–0	Barmby 24, Gascoigne 25, Shearer 61	9,500
9.10.96	Poland	Wembley	W	2–1	Shearer 24, 38	74,663
9.11.96	Georgia	Tbilisi	W	2–0	Sheringham 15, Ferdinand 37	48,000
12.2.97	Italy	Wembley	L	0–1		75,055
30.4.97	Georgia	Wembley	W	2–0	Sheringham 43, Shearer 90	71,208
31.5.97	Poland	Chorzow	W	2–0	Shearer 6, Sheringham 90	35,000
10.9.97	Moldova	Wembley	W	4–0	Scholes 28, Wright 46, 90, Gascoigne 81	74,102
11.10.97	Italy	Rome	D	0–0		81,200

APPEARANCES AND GOALSCORERS			
Player	Apps	Subs	Goals
Tony Adams	3		
Nicky Barmby	1		1
David Batty	5	2	
David Beckham	8		
Nicky Butt	–	2	
Sol Campbell	6		
Stan Collymore	–	1	
Les Ferdinand	3	1	1
Paul Gascoigne	6		2
Andy Hinchcliffe	3		
Paul Ince	7		
Graeme Le Saux	4		
Matt Le Tissier	1	1	
Robert Lee	2		
Steve McManaman	2		
Paul Merson	–	1	
Gary Neville	6		
Phil Neville	1	1	
Gary Pallister	1	1	
Stuart Pearce	3		
Jamie Redknapp	–	1	
Stuart Ripley	–	1	
Paul Scholes	1		1
David Seaman	7		
Alan Shearer	5		5
Teddy Sheringham	4		3
Gareth Southgate	6	1	
Ian Walker	1		
Ian Wright	2	2	2

**We've done it!
Hoddle and Gascoigne
celebrate in Rome.**

GOALS BREAKDOWN	
Scored at home	8
Scored away	7
Conceded at home	2
Conceded away	0

WHEN GOALS CAME		
	For	Conceded
0–15 mins	1	1
15–30 mins	5	1
30–45 mins	3	0
45–60 mins	1	0
60–75 mins	1	0
75–90 mins	4	0

Chapter 2
Prospects for France

Complete the following sequence: 1966, England; 1970, Brazil; 1974, West Germany; 1978, Argentina; 1982, Italy; 1986, Argentina; 1990, Germany; 1994, Brazil; 1998, – ? If you put "England", congratulations, your Mensa membership card is in the post.

Now try this one for size: 1986, quarter-finals; 1990, semi-finals; 1998, –? You've guessed it. If good omens are anything to go by, England will be there, on July 12, in the final of the World Cup.

But first, there is the small matter of three group games to negotiate, followed – hopefully – by a second-round match, a quarter-final and a semi-final. The first-round draw was relatively kind to England, but no one in manager Glenn Hoddle's camp will underestimate Colombia, Romania and Tunisia, who all pose their own particular threats in Group G.

England are drawn against Tunisia, Romania and Colombia in the World Cup draw in Marseille.

What happens next is anybody's guess. But the traditional heavyweights of the game, along with one or two dark horses, are sure to have their say in the subsequent rounds.

Rising to the challenge

It's a formidable challenge, but England are more than capable of rising to the occasion. They won Le Tournoi last summer, finishing ahead of Brazil, France and Italy and acclimatizing to France's stadiums and facilities, and their irresistible form in the qualifiers forced the rest of the world's footballing superpowers to sit up and take notice.

"It's eight years since we last qualified for the finals," says Hoddle. "And we've given the country fantastic enjoyment in getting there. We're growing as a squad and that's because we've done so well away from home off the back of playing at Wembley throughout Euro 96."

This summer, France is the place to be. The 16th World Cup promises to be the biggest and best yet, with more countries taking part than ever before and more TV viewers tuning in to watch the greatest show on earth. With France virtually on the doorstep, Hoddle's men can also expect fantastic support from their own fans, many of whom are too young to remember the last time an English footballer held the glittering trophy aloft in celebration.

Of course, no one can legislate for the myriad of unforeseen mishaps – like injuries and loss of form – that a tournament like the World Cup can throw up. Players can pick up knocks in the opening matches, and needless cautions can rule them out of the later stages. But England will not fail for lack of effort or self-belief. For the first time in a long time, the national team is oozing confidence on the eve of the finals – and playing like a club side. The squad is packed full of talented individuals whose versatile, attractive brand of football has won nothing but praise, and in Hoddle they have a young, innovative coach who has the utmost faith in his players and his own powers of motivation.

"The hard work starts now," he declares. "We set ourselves standards in the qualifiers and we want to do well when we get to France."

Can his England team really win the World Cup? "Give me my best players," he says, "Give me my best team. And possibly, just possibly." The countdown starts here.

Paul Ince: dynamic as ever at Le Tournoi.

Group G rivals

It could have been worse – a lot worse.

When Sepp Blatter, the General Secretary of FIFA, commenced the draw for the first round of the World Cup finals in Marseille on December 4, last year, there was a fair chance that England would find themselves in the same group as Brazil or Argentina. Instead, they got Romania, one of the least fancied of the top seeds, along with Colombia and Tunisia in Group G. Glenn Hoddle grinned. He seemed reasonably happy and quietly confident.

Why, though, weren't England one of the top seeds – like, for example, the country which finished second to them in their qualifying group? Blame it on the seeding system, which is based on form in the last

Robert Lee reinforced his first-team claims with a goal against South Africa in May 1997.

three World Cup tournaments. England, of course, failed to qualify for the 1994 tournament in the USA, but Italy reached the final.

Prior to the draw, there was speculation that FIFA might change the system to include their own world rankings, introduced in 1993, in which England had reached an all-time high of sixth. But the world governing body stuck to its guns and split the competing nations into four tiers of eight. Hence the top tier consisted of Brazil, Italy, Germany, Argentina, Spain, Belgium, Romania and France (as hosts).

The complex draw heralded the 16th and biggest World Cup finals of all time. The facts and figures are staggering. This summer, 32 nations will play 64 games over 32 days in 10 stadiums – the most impressive being the new £223 million, 80,000-capacity Grande Stade in the Saint Denis district of Paris – watched by a total projected TV audience of 37 billion. FIFA estimate that it will cost £273 million to stage the tournament – £96 million more than USA '94.

Between March 10, 1996, and November 29, 1997, it took 645 matches between 168 countries to decide who would compete in the last, great sporting spectacle of the millennium. England earned their place there – and they could go far.

No pushovers

They kick off their group against Tunisia in Marseille on June 15. African teams can be unpredictable, and the Tunisians are no exception. Ranked 23rd by FIFA, they have never been past the first round, but they won their qualifying group and were narrowly beaten by South Africa, who had home advantage, in the final of the 1996 African Nations Cup.

England have played against them just once: in a World Cup warm-up in June 1990, they drew 1–1 in Tunis, with a last-minute equalizer by Steve Bull saving

Marseille: venue for England's opening game.

On to Toulouse – and a tough test against Romania.

Bobby Robson's blushes. Tunisia's top players in 1998 are Adel Sellimi, a lively left-sided forward capped a record 50 times, and his striking partner Mehdi Slimane.

On paper, it appears to be the least demanding of England's first-round matches, but there are other factors to consider. Marseille is quite close to the Tunisian coast, and the North Africans will have a large presence among the 60,000 crowd in the newly-refurbished Stade Vélodrome, the second-largest stadium in France. Glenn Hoddle will also be aware of the region's humid, Mediterranean climate and its effect upon his players. In a knock-out tournament such as this, nothing can be left to chance.

Top seeds and dark horses

A week later, England face Romania in another southern venue, Toulouse. Ranked fifth in the world, and an outside bet of 40 to 1 to win the competition, the Eastern Europeans are a match for anyone on their day. They were unbeaten in their qualifying group, winning nine matches and drawing one. But the Republic of Ireland, Macedonia, Lithuania, Iceland and Liechtenstein hardly provided world-class opposition.

There is a feeling that the Romanians are past their best. The stars who shone so brightly in the USA in 1994 – especially in the scintillating second-round victory over Argentina – are in the twilight of their careers and perhaps not the force they once were. Coach Anghel Iordanescu's team of far-flung footballers is built around ageing playmaker Gheorghe Hagi, famously dubbed the "Maradona of the Carpathians", and there is a Premiership presence in Chelsea's Dan Petrescu and Viorel Moldovan of Coventry City. In nine previous encounters between the two countries, England have lost just once – way back in 1980 in Bucharest. The most recent meeting, in October 1994, produced a 1–1 draw at Wembley.

Notorious underachievers

England's final match in the group pits them against Colombia in Lens on 26 June. It promises to be an absorbing contest: Glenn Hoddle's new, improved England against one of South America's more erratic countries.

Despite their undoubted talents, the Colombians are notorious underachievers. One of the tournament favourites in 1994, they were a huge disappointment, finishing bottom in a first-round group that featured Romania, Switzerland and the USA.

This is their third successive appearance in the finals, and so far they have never been beyond the last 16. Like Romania, the team revolves around one player – 36-year-old skipper Carlos Valderrama – although there is, of course, a more familiar danger up front. Former Newcastle striker Faustino Asprilla is a formidable opponent, and his old team-mate Robert Lee is taking nothing for granted.

The England midfielder warns, "It's hard to plan how to play against him because you can't predict what he's going to do next or what he's thinking."

Colombia finished third behind Argentina and Paraguay in the South American qualifiers and are ranked ninth in the world by FIFA. They have failed to beat England in three previous encounters, but did enough during the goalless friendly at Wembley in September 1995 to suggest that they are a force to be reckoned with.

Hoddle's side, however, may have a slight advan-

Shearer strikes in the win over France at Le Tournoi

Lens: a 'homely' setting for England's third game.

tage in terms of playing conditions. Lens, a coal-mining town in the heart of the Artois district, is the most northerly of France's World Cup venues with a very "English" climate. It's a long haul from Toulouse to Lens in the space of four days, but England can take comfort from the fact that they are playing Colombia in the evening in a compact stadium with a famously friendly atmosphere.

Climatic concerns

In Mexico in 1986, England had to cope with both the excessive heat and altitude. Even the finals in Italy four years later posed problems, with Bobby Robson's men confined to Sardinia for the opening stages. The World Cup is a summer tournament, and perhaps this gives South American countries an edge.

A few years ago, former Brazilian star Carlos Alberto remarked, "In England, football is played on the pitches of winter. It should be played in the summer. In Brazil we play more or less all the year round and on some very dry and very bad pitches. But it produces some very good players."

Nevertheless, European countries traditionally perform well on European soil – Brazil are the only South American team to win the World Cup in Europe – and the relative proximity of France, along with its typically European weather and excellent infrastructure, should work in England's favour.

For the first time in World Cup history, the competing nations will be required to play their first-round matches in different venues across the country, but Hoddle's squad, of course, has already had a taste of tournament football in France. Le Tournoi was important not just as a test of strength against three of

the world's top teams, but also as a warm-up for the real thing. On that occasion, England passed with flying colours, and the experience gained from travelling between Nantes, Montpellier and Paris last year will prove invaluable. Hoddle even intends to use the same training camp in north-west France.

One thing is certain: the playing surfaces will be as smooth as bowling greens. Former French skipper Michel Platini, a member of the country's World Cup organising committee, has unhappy memories of the bumpy pitches in Argentina in 1978 and has demanded only the very best from his country's groundsmen. France, which first hosted the finals way back in 1938 and also staged the 1984 European Championships, is determined to provide the finest facilities in the competition's long and illustrious history.

Demand outstrips supply

But just how many England fans will be there to enjoy them? Initially, only 20 per cent of all tickets for the finals were allocated to non-French fans. The English FA received 5,000 tickets for the match against Tunisia, 3,000 for the Romania game and just 2,500 for the showdown with Colombia, all of which were priced between 145 and 350 francs (roughly £14.50 and £35.00 at end-1997 exchange rates) and were only available to the 27,000 people in the England Members Club – a membership which was more than five times greater than that of England's highest ticket allocation.

Demand has far exceeded supply. The French organizing committee have already received more than 500,000 requests for tickets for the final on July 12. The FA have fielded 200 calls a day since England secured their qualification, and the day after the draw was made all four British Airways flights to Marseille on June 14 and 15 – when England play Tunisia – were sold out.

An FA spokesman admitted, "A lot of people are going to be disappointed."

That said, the FA asked to be kept informed of any developments. Glenn Hoddle made a point of thanking England's followers for their support during the qualifier against Italy in Rome, and his team will be counting on their tremendous backing and encouragement in France, where England are sure to be one of the best-supported teams in the tournament.

Above all, Hoddle's squad will approach the finals

brimming with confidence. There have been moods of optimism before – notably in Mexico in 1970, when Alf Ramsey's reigning world champions were accused of being over-confident, even complacent, going into their fateful quarter-final with West Germany.

Twenty years later, England seemed to have learned from their mistakes. Bobby Robson's team reached the 1990 finals by winning three and drawing three of their qualifiers during a run of 17 matches without defeat. After a modest start, they improved as the tournament progressed and more than matched the Germans in the semi-finals before going out on penalties.

As it is, they are joint-third favourites with Germany and Italy to win the World Cup. If England win their group, there is a good chance that they will face Croatia in the second round. If they reach the Final, it's likely that they will have played Germany and Italy or France to get there. The prospect of facing any or all of these countries should not hold any fears. With so many foreigners in the cosmopolitan Premiership – many of them certain to feature in the finals – Hoddle's players are well-versed in the wiles of continental football. In fact, this is arguably the best-equipped England World Cup squad since 1966,

Three lions on a shirt: England's support in France will be crucial.

This time, however, there is a genuine feeling among the England squad that they are good enough to go all the way.

Graeme Le Saux sums up the mood in the camp: "You need something extra to be successful. It's like an aura, you become protective of each other. We're all hard workers. If I have to make that extra run, I do it without thinking. I can think of three players who could take my place and that gives you an edge, which is healthy."

when home advantage undoubtedly played its part.

Admittedly, a team like Brazil, boasting the glittering talents of Ronaldo, the world's most expensive footballer, are a different proposition altogether. But while Hoddle was quick to acknowledge their genius at Le Tournoi, he insisted that England should not feel inferior. "There is still a gap between us and Brazil," he said. "But it's a gap that can be bridged. There are things we're good at but they're poor at. But they've also got things in their game that we need to put into ours."

(left) Ronaldo, the world's most expensive footballer, dances through the England defence at Le Tournoi.

(below) Robert Lee: one of England's new breed of versatile footballers.

Adapting to the modern game

Twenty-eight years ago, when Brazil thrilled the world with a breathtaking exhibition of football in Mexico, the legendary Pele made an intriguing comment about the difference between the South American and European games: "Our football comes from the heart, theirs comes from the mind."

His statement still holds true, but there are signs in England's football that Hoddle is trying to strike a balance between both philosophies. England have never been short on passion and fighting spirit – as foreign observers are so fond of telling us – but the team has also acquired a new technical and tactical dimension, and it is often described as playing "intelligent" football. Take the sweeper system, for so long an alien concept to English players.

"I'm sure I speak for Gary Neville and Sol Campbell when I say using the deeper-lying sweeper is an enjoyable way to play," reveals centre-half Gareth Southgate. "It's proved very effective because you need that extra depth and cover when defending against top-quality players, as you can't gamble on the offside trap at this level and you need players who are quick. It certainly suits our personnel."

The result is a happy and, above all, comfortable group of players willing to listen and adapt to the coach's ideas. Listen to Carlos Alberto now: "Hoddle's team is the best England team I've seen. Once they were a bit one-dimensional, but now they play more skilfully, composed and balanced. They can combine speed, technique and, for the first time, adapt to different styles and patterns."

Of course, every team needs a talisman, especially one who scores plenty of goals. "If you're going to win the World Cup, you need a consistent goalscorer like Rossi or Maradona," admits Hoddle. "We've got players who are capable of scoring from other areas but to have an out-and-out scorer is vital for a tournament like this."

Alan Shearer is the obvious candidate – he was top scorer in Euro 96 – but when the £15 million man was injured last year England learned to cope without him. Hoddle has always enjoyed a wealth of options in attack – hence the run-outs for Paul Scholes and Robbie Fowler, among others, in England's friendly against Cameroon last November. Both players scored in the 2–0 victory at Wembley that night, and both put themselves in contention for a place in the squad.

The coach must have a firm idea of his team for the finals, but he has made every effort to fine-tune his system and experiment with new combinations and faces. Already, England's future stars are learning how to adapt to the demands of international football.

Winning the World Cup will require a superhuman effort – neither Hoddle nor his squad are under any illusions about that. But the country can rest assured England's players will be straining every sinew to bring the trophy back after an absence of 28 years.

French coach Aimé Jacquet, for one, is warning the world to watch out for the three lions. "Glenn Hoddle has obviously developed a new style and their progress has been amazing," he says. "It wouldn't surprise me if they have a good World Cup, especially after their excellent performance at Le Tournoi. In fact, it wouldn't surprise me at all."

WORLD CUP 1997			
GROUP G			
June 15	**England vs. Tunisia**	Marseille	1.30pm
June 15	**Romania vs. Colombia**	Lyon	4.30pm
June 22	**Colombia vs. Tunisia**	Montpellier	4.30pm
June 22	**Romania vs. England**	Toulouse	8pm
June 26	**Romania vs. Tunisia**	Saint Denis	8pm
June 26	**Colombia vs. England**	Lens	8pm

GROUP A
Brazil, Morocco, Norway, Scotland

GROUP B
Austria, Cameroon, Chile, Italy

GROUP C
Denmark, France, Saudi Arabia, South Africa

GROUP D
Bulgaria, Nigeria, Paraguay, Spain

GROUP E
Belgium, Holland, Mexico, South Korea

GROUP F
Germany, Iran, USA, Yugoslavia

GROUP H
Argentina, Croatia, Jamaica, Japan

Second Round

There are tie-breaks if two teams end on the same number of points – three for a win, one for a draw – at the end of the First Round (group stage) for qualification into the knock-out rounds:

1. **Goal difference**
2. **Goals scored**
3. **Result of game between the two teams**
4. **Coin toss**

If England win their group, they will play the runners-up from Group H in Bordeaux on June 30 at 3.30 pm.

If England are runners-up, they will play the winners from Group H in St Etienne on June 30 at 8pm.

If the teams are level at the end of 90 minutes, the "Golden Goal" rule comes into effect, i.e. the first goal wins. If no goal is scored after 30 minutes, there is a penalty shoot-out.

(All kick-off times BST. France is one hour ahead of England, so England vs. Tunisia will kick-off at 2.30 pm in Marseille.)

Robbie Fowler stakes a late claim with a goal in the friendly against Mexico in March 1997. Hoddle has always been ready to give youth its head.

Chapter 3
England's Star Players

Glenn Hoddle used 29 players in England's eight qualifying World Cup matches. All of them played their part, but sadly at least eight of them will be missing from his 22-man squad for the finals.

Never can a national coach have been so spoilt for choice, such is the quantity and quality of talent available to him. No wonder England are rated at 7–1 to win the tournament for a second time.

The men who will make the cut possess ability in abundance. With the greatest of respect to the boys of '66, this is arguably the most accomplished England squad ever to grace the World Cup, and most encouraging of all is the self-belief which pervades throughout it. England, ranked sixth by FIFA at the turn of the year, have proved that they can match the best in the world.

Hoddle's England play like a club side, rather than a group of strangers who meet up once in a while for internationals. "At Le Tournoi," says the coach, "I had the chance to have a look at different players."

The result is a set of players aware of each other's strengths, used to winning and supremely versatile. During the first two years of Hoddle's reign, the balance of the side has been maintained despite the use of different personnel.

Talent in every position

In David Seaman, the coach has one of the finest goalkeepers in the world. In front of him, whether operating a flat back-four or sweeper system, England's defenders are becoming more and more comfortable on the ball without losing their traditional values of grit and determination.

Wright and Batty share a joke during training.

In midfield, the quality of players is staggering; alongside the invaluable experience of Paul Gascoigne and Paul Ince is the youthful exuberance of players like David Beckham and Steve McManaman. The coach, of course, has never been afraid to give youth its head.

"Age isn't what we're talking about," he argues. "I've never equated experience with grey hairs. Some players spend all their careers making the wrong decisions. You can be experienced at doing the wrong thing. You can also be properly experienced at 25."

Up front, he has an embarrassment of riches. "I make no bones about it," he adds. "I want Alan Shearer fit. But we've shown that we can cope without him. We don't have to create 10 chances to score a goal. One of the bonuses of being England coach at the moment is the quality of the goalscorers available."

Overall, it's the perfect blend: emerging stars, many of them from Manchester United, eager to make their mark on the international stage, and a clutch of veterans determined to make up for lost time and take England all the way. Eight years have come and gone since England last graced the World Cup finals, but it could be worth the wait.

The statistics in the following chapter cover games up to February 12, 1998.

Alan Shearer and David Beckham watch and learn from Paul Gascoigne, England's most talented star.

Tim **Flowers**

It's not easy being an understudy goalkeeper at international level, especially for England. Over the years, an elite band of individuals have monopolized the Number 1 jersey.

Between them, Gordon Banks, Ray Clemence and Peter Shilton amassed 259 caps, and Arsenal's David Seaman is well on his way to reaching the 50 mark. But Tim Flowers is a patient man, and at 31 years of age he still has plenty of time to make the position his own.

He also has plenty to boast about. He became Britain's most expensive goalkeeper, when he joined Blackburn for £2.4 million from Southampton in 1993.

Flowers has played twice against Brazil no less – making his debut in a summer tournament in the USA in 1993 and in the 1995 Umbro Cup tournament. Who knows, his experience in those two matches might just come in handy should the reigning world champions cross England's path in France.

Tim Flowers: patience is an essential requirement for any would-be England goalkeeper.

No room for complacency

Even as Seaman's deputy, however, Flowers knows that there is no room for complacency. He played at Le Tournoi, but a double hernia operation caused him to drop out of the squad for the subsequent World Cup qualifier against Moldova at Wembley – and there was no shortage of replacements eager to grab themselves a slice of the action.

As always – and despite the falling ratio of English to foreign goalkeepers in the Premiership – competition for the national team jersey is fierce, with both Tottenham's Ian Walker and Nigel Martyn of Leeds United staking serious claims for a place in the squad, though the former appears out of favour with Hoddle at the moment.

But as a shotstopper, Flowers is second to none, and his athleticism, reflexes and agility played a big part in Blackburn's League campaign in 1995. It was a season which ended in triumph but nearly began in disaster.

During one of his first pre-season training sessions with Blackburn, he fell awkwardly on a goalpost peg which pierced his arm and ripped his muscles. He required seven stitches in a gash on his elbow. But he's no stranger, it would appear, to incidents of a bizarre nature.

"Five years ago, I celebrated that first appearance against Brazil on my debut with a bit of a radical haircut," he explains. "When Graham Taylor picked me two days before the game, there was a mixture of elation and nerves. It was hard to sink in that it was me, Tim Flowers, playing for England against Brazil. I just wanted to tell everyone. But as the match drew closer, I became more and more nervous.

"At the time, a bloke in the hotel where we were staying kept urging me, Paul Merson and Lee Sharpe to have our hair cut. I was the guinea pig and the others followed suit. It cost us £20 each. After the match, I rang home to talk to my folks. The first thing my dad said was, 'What do you think you look like?'."

There's just no pleasing some people!

Tim FLOWERS

Position: Goalkeeper
Place of birth: Kenilworth
Date of birth: February 3, 1967
Height: 6ft 3in
Weight: 14st 4lb
Clubs: Wolverhampton Wanderers, Southampton, Blackburn Rovers
International debut: Brazil, June 13, 1993
Appearances: 9
Goals: 0

David **Seaman**

David Seaman: coolness personified in the epic 0–0 draw with Italy that secured a World Cup spot.

David SEAMAN

Position: Goalkeeper
Place of birth: Rotherham
Date of birth: September 19, 1963
Height: 6ft 4in
Weight: 14st 10lb
Clubs: Leeds United, Peterborough United, Birmingham City, Queens Park Rangers, Arsenal
International debut: Saudi Arabia (A), November 16, 1988
Appearances: 38
Goals: 0

It was the moment when millions of English hearts skipped a beat. In the dying seconds in Rome, Italy launched one last, frantic assault on the visitors' goal. As the England defence back-pedalled, a cross from the left was met firmly by the head of Christian Vieri, and 81,200 pairs of eyes in the Stadio Olimpico watched as the ball looped, as if in slow-motion, toward goal... and just wide of it.

While the Italians in the stands tore out their hair in anguish, David Seaman flicked back his own impec-cably-styled locks and retrieved the ball for the goal-kick. At the final whistle, he jogged over to Glenn Hoddle, grinned and shrugged. "It's okay, boss," he said. "I knew it was going wide."

What a contrast to the last time Seaman was involved in a make-or-break World Cup qualifier. Back in October 1993, a crafty free-kick from Ronald Koeman sailed inside his right-hand post and helped book Holland's place in the finals in the USA at England's expense. The jovial Yorkshire giant took more than his fair share of criticism for that soul-destroying result, and it is a tribute to his profession-alism and consistency that he remains England's undisputed Number One and has since become a national hero, to boot.

Super spot-kick saver

In the 1996 European Championships, Alan Shearer may have grabbed the goals, but it was Seaman who captured the country's hearts after his penalty saves against Scotland in the first round and Spain in the quarter-finals.

His displays in the 1994 World Cup qualifying cam-paign were less dramatic but just as immaculate. Seaman conceded just one goal in seven matches – in the 2–1 Wembley win over Poland – and may just have kept another clean-sheet in the home showdown with Italy had a cartilage injury not kept him on the sidelines.

Like every great goalkeeper, he has matured with age. He was 25 and had been transferred three times – from Leeds (without making a first-team appearance) to Peterborough to Birmingham to QPR – before he won his first cap for England in 1988. But it wasn't until Arsenal lured him away from Loftus Road in a £1.3 million deal two years later that he began to establish himself as the top goalkeeper in the country, winning Championship, FA Cup and European Cup-winner's Cup medals in the process.

Ever the perfectionist, Seaman trains daily with for-mer Arsenal goalkeeper Bob Wilson and is always seeking to improve his game. He has even had a set of floodlights at Highbury tilted at a different angle because their glare was affecting his performance on crosses in midweek matches.

The third-most capped member of the England squad (behind Tony Adams and Paul Gascoigne), the 34-year-old will bring all his experience to bear in his first World Cup. Whatever obstacles await his team-mates in France, they can rest assured that they have England's safest pair of hands behind them.

Gary Neville

If Gary Neville has a fault, it's that he's too modest. Take his verdict on playing as a wing-back:

"It's my least favourite position. I can beat players going forward, but there are better players than me in that position. I've been told I've got to be more positive, but sometimes I think I've got this mentality that I am a defender first and a footballer second. My brother Phil is good at making the decision about when to go forward. Maybe I'm a bit too cautious."

Over to Glenn Hoddle: "I don't agree with him at all. Look at the cross he provided for Alan Shearer's goal against Scotland in Euro 96. He's got a very mature head and he's an accomplished player at a very young age with a lot of experience under his belt."

He might not think it, but Neville looks comfortable in any position. As well as occupying the wing-back berth, he has played at full-back and centre-half for England.

Along with his versatility, he possesses the right sort of big-match temperament. He played in six of England's World Cup qualifying matches, and with each game he grew in stature. In the return match against Poland, in particular, he was outstanding.

Always keen to play

Just as pleasing for Hoddle is Gary's enthusiasm for international duty. After another glorious but demanding season with Manchester United, the defender could have been excused for feeling a little tired. Instead, he was itching to board the plane to France for Le Tournoi.

"You can't play roulette," he said at the time. "You can't go around saying, 'I think I'll miss this tournament or this game.' After all, I might never get another chance to play against Brazil."

And let's get another thing straight: Gary travelled to France with Alex Ferguson's blessing. "The manager has never said to me that he's going to pull me out

Gary NEVILLE	
Position: Full-back	
Place of birth: Bury	
Date of birth: February 18, 1975	
Height: 5ft 10in	
Weight: 11st 10lb	
Clubs: Manchester United	
International debut: Japan (H), June 3, 1995	
Appearances: 24	
Goals: 0	

of an England game," says Gary. "If a young player needs a rest at United, he'll be given a rest and we all put our trust in him to make that choice. If I'm in the England squad, we don't even have a conversation about it. I just go. He doesn't have any problem with any of us playing for England."

To date, Gary's career has been little short of sensational. He made his Manchester United debut aged 19 and, like his younger brother, made his first England appearance against Oriental opposition: just 12 days after featuring in the 1995 FA Cup Final against Everton, he played in the Umbro Cup against Japan.

"Sometimes people ask me if I think I'm too young to be put in these situations," he reflects. "But, for some people, it never happens, so how can you be too young? You're only going to get experience by playing in big games. Handling situations is part of being a Manchester United player."

And, it seems, being a fully established England defender, whatever position he finds himself in.

Gary Neville: Since making his debut against Japan in 1995 he has matured into a fine player.

Phil Neville: Following closely in his older brother's footsteps, he shows much promise.

Phil **Neville**

Anything Gary can do, Phil can do, too. In fact, Phil can do it quicker. The younger of Manchester United's Neville boys made his first senior appearance for England aged 19. His big brother didn't make his debut until he was 20.

If it hadn't been for a rotten spell of luck with injury and illness, Phil might have had just as many caps to his name as Gary. After making his debut alongside Gary in a friendly against China (becoming the first brothers to play for England since Bobby and Jack Charlton) and receiving a call-up from Terry Venables for the Euro 1996 squad, Phil underwent an ankle operation, sustained a hamstring injury and contracted glandular fever, all in the space of a few months. It was a frightening experience, and he lost a

stone-and-a-half in the process.

"I couldn't speak and I couldn't walk at times," he reveals. "It was too painful. My best friend had glandular fever a few years ago and he was out for the whole season, so it was very worrying. Normally it's one injury a season. To be out for six weeks then be back for three only to be injured again was very frustrating."

Change of fortune

A year later, his luck changed dramatically. After a storming performance at Le Tournoi, he came on as a second-half substitute for David Beckham in the World Cup qualifier in Poland and kept his place for the 4–0 drubbing of Moldova at Wembley. Strong, pacey and comfortable on either flank, he is now an established international with the world at his feet.

It was Phil's remarkable form in the summer tournament in France that really caught the eye. Against Italy, he defended resolutely, scorched down the wing at every opportunity and whipped over some great crosses. In the final match against Brazil, he more than held his own against the formidable Roberto Carlos in a taxing 90 minutes. Glenn Hoddle, for one, was mightily impressed.

Not that Phil's rapid progress should come as any surprise. Sporting excellence is something of a tradition in the Neville household. Phil's twin, Tracey, is an international netball player and their father is a coach at Bury. One thing Phil and Gary are not, however, is competitive – at least not with each other.

> **Phil NEVILLE**
> **Position:** Full-back
> **Place of birth:** Bury
> **Date of birth:** January 21, 1977
> **Height:** 5ft 10in
> **Weight:** 11st 10lb
> **Clubs:** Manchester United
> **International debut:** China (A), May 23, 1996
> **Appearances:** 9
> **Goals:** 0

"If I had to pick the team, Gary would be in it every time and *vice versa*," insists Phil. "I'll always want Gary to do well. I remember a couple of seasons ago, I was playing in the United team for a spell and Gary wasn't. People kept coming up and asking me how it felt to keep him out of the side. But I wasn't keeping him out. Gary is a right-back and Dennis Irwin was playing in his position. I was on the other flank. So it was Dennis who was keeping him out of the team. That's the way we both looked at it."

Sibling rivalry? More like brotherly love!

Graeme Le Saux

Graeme Le Saux: Proud to wear the England jersey.

Ruptured ligaments, a dislocation of the right ankle and a spiral fracture of the fibula. Oh, and a broken elbow thrown in for good measure. Graeme Le Saux has recovered from them all, which only goes to prove that you can't keep a world-class full-back down.

It's over two years since his world caved in during a match between Blackburn Rovers and Middlesbrough at Ewood Park. At the time, he was England's established left-back and the draw for the European Championship finals was to be made the next day. But an accidental challenge by Boro's Brazilian midfielder Juninho left him writhing in agony and out of action for the best part of a year.

"I was running one way and tried to check," he recalls. "As I turned, he just caught me. My foot got planted in the soil and all my weight went through my ankle. My initial reaction was, 'Will I ever play again?' When you look down the front of your leg and over your knee and see your heel sticking out, you know that there is something seriously wrong."

The injury was almost identical to the one which would sideline Alan Shearer in August 1997. Le Saux likened his sudden, violent lay-off to being thrown from a car on the motorway and watching as it speeds off into the distance. While his England colleagues geared up for Euro 96, he was put in plaster and had a metal plate and six screws inserted in his ankle. Stuart Pearce, the old campaigner whom Le Saux had succeeded in the England side, replaced him for the tournament.

Graeme LE SAUX	
Position:	Full-back
Place of birth:	Jersey
Date of birth:	October, 17, 1968
Height:	5ft 10in
Weight:	12st 2lb
Clubs:	Chelsea, Blackburn Rovers, Chelsea
International debut:	Denmark (H), March 9, 1994
Appearances:	22
Goals:	1

Long rehabilitation

Not once, however, did Le Saux let his disappointment get the better of him. He was out of plaster after eight weeks and, slowly but surely, his rehabilitation took him out of the treatment room and back into the Blackburn first team. An England recall followed in 1997 – plus a surprise £5 million return to his old club Chelsea – and he was one of the most consistent performers in the World Cup qualifying campaign.

Le Saux seems certain to feature prominently in Glenn Hoddle's plans this summer, either as a conventional left-back or a more attack-minded wing-back. After the trials and tribulations that the likeable Channel Islander has been through, winning the World Cup must seem like a doddle.

"England is very important to me," Le Saux said. "I have tried to look at it as a reward for playing well for my club. When I got injured, I realized just how short the length of your career could be." Now back in one piece, Le Saux, more than anyone else in the England squad, will be making the most of France 98.

Tony **Adams**

When Dutch referee Mario van der Ende blew the final whistle in Rome's Stadio Olimpico on October 11, 1997, all hell broke loose among the elated England party. Qualification was assured and Glenn Hoddle's coaching staff leapt up, hugged each other and danced a jig of joy. On the pitch, tears flowed down cheeks and fists punched the air.

Graeme Le Saux later described the scenes back in the dressing-room: "It was a mixture of feelings. Some people were excited; we had to strap Ian Wright down! But Tony Adams stayed very calm. I suppose people express their feelings in different ways."

Once upon a time, the Arsenal skipper would have led the celebrations. But Adams is a changed man. It is almost two years since he stood up in the Highbury dressing-room and confessed to team-mates that he was an alcoholic. His courage and determination to rebuild his career have subsequently made him a firm favourite with football fans around the country.

"I don't have mood-swings so much these days – like getting tremendous highs after games when we've won, or tremendous lows when we've lost," he reveals. "I'm a lot more balanced. My philosophy now is that I do the best I can for me, and by doing the best for me I'm helping everyone else. Maybe the screaming and shouting and clenched fists were a way of trying to impress people, to show that I cared. But I care anyway. The feelings are all inside now, but perhaps the desire is even greater."

The elder statesman

On his 48th appearance for his country – he is one of a select band of England internationals who have played under Bobby Robson, Graham Taylor, Terry Venables and Glenn Hoddle – Adams was a colossus. To ease the pressure on the towering centre-half, Hoddle gave the captaincy to Paul Ince on the night, but as usual Adams led by example, marshalling his defence superbly and showing remarkable calm when Italian striker Alessandro Del Piero tried desperately to win a penalty off him in the closing stages of the match.

At the age of 31, it was a remarkable performance by a player who has endured more ups and downs during his long career than he cares to remember. Under Hoddle and his Arsenal boss Arsène Wenger, he has matured into one of the most accomplished defenders in the country.

Although the limbs may be getting a little stiffer after matches – Wenger ordered him to have a short period of complete rest last season to recover from a niggling injury – he remains rock-solid, ultra-reliable and more than capable of competing against some of the deadliest marksmen in the world.

After all, four consecutive England coaches can't be wrong.

Tony ADAMS

Position: Centre-half
Place of birth: London
Date of birth: October 10, 1966
Height: 6ft 3in
Weight: 13st 11lb
Clubs: Arsenal
International debut: Spain (A), February 18, 1987
Appearances: 49
Goals: 4

Tony Adams: the rock on which England is built.

Sol Campbell

Sol Campbell had his Tottenham team-mates in stitches when he made his first appearance in an England shirt two years ago.

Not because of the way he played, but because of the opposition. Spurs veteran David Howells explains: "Sol is a big lad with an incredible appetite. I've never seen anyone eat so much in my life. So you can imagine what a laugh we had when he made his debut. It just had to be against Hungary!"

Campbell stands 6ft 1in tall. But he will never grow as much as he did in the days that followed England's World Cup qualifying defeat by Italy in February 1997. Barely a quarter of an hour into the game, a pass from Alessandro Costacurta split the England defence, allowing Gianfranco Zola to burst through and beat Ian Walker at his near post. Campbell, the nearest England player to the goalscorer, admitted after the match that he had made a "positioning" mistake, and the press duly took him to the cleaners.

Learning from mistakes

He was too honest for his own good. "That game made me as a player because I learned so much on the day and in the weeks after," he reflects. "It was incredible how much I learned."

In truth, he had done little wrong in what was only his second full international and one that he describes as his "best passing performance" for England. Glenn Hoddle was inclined to agree. Campbell stayed in the squad and had established himself as first-choice centre-half by the end of the domestic season.

"From the time we played the friendly against South Africa to the World Cup match in Poland and the summer tournament in France, we were together for about 20 days," he recalls. "I think when a set of players has been away together for a long time, you learn a lot about each other. The lads have been through a lot together now. You feel more comfortable with

Sol Campbell: still learning the England ropes.

the people around you."

By the time England resumed hostilities with Italy in Rome, the Tottenham defender was a tower of strength at the back and hardly put a foot wrong all evening, snuffing out the dual threat of Zola and Enrico Chiesa and forcing Italian midfielder Angelo di Livio to make a tackle that produced a red card. Not bad for a 23-year-old winning his 11th cap.

"Before the game, you could sense we were all ready for it," he reveals. "It's funny because as the qualifying games went on, we tended to do a few things to lighten the atmosphere, like mucking around with the ball in the dressing room.

"But you could tell that, this time, everyone was totally, totally focused. There was no messing about. All our minds were working together."

Having survived such an ordeal, he's ready for anything in France. "Whether it's Italy, Brazil or whoever, everyone is human," says England's human food dispenser. "That's all you've got to remember."

Sol CAMPBELL	
Position:	Centre-half
Place of birth:	Newham, London
Date of birth:	September 18, 1974
Height:	6ft 1in
Weight:	14st 1lb
Clubs:	Tottenham Hotspur
International debut:	Hungary (H), May 18, 1996
Appearances:	13
Goals:	0

Rio **Ferdinand**

There were 46,176 spectators at Wembley Stadium when Rio Ferdinand came on as a 39th-minute substitute for Gareth Southgate in last year's friendly against Cameroon. In years to come, of course, at least five times that number will say they were there when "the new Bobby Moore" made his senior debut for England. The elegant, ball-playing centre-half is surely destined for great things.

"Rio is the player this country has been waiting for," says West Ham manager Harry Redknapp. But Ferdinand so nearly slipped through the net as a youngster. He was more interested in athletics and gymnastics than football, and only a chance turn-out in midfield for his uncle's local team in Peckham, south London, put him on the road to stardom.

Within a month, he was spotted by a scout and

Rio Ferdinand: still a teenager but the West Ham defender could be a future England captain.

snapped up by QPR, with whom he spent three years before joining the Hammers. "Everybody there was really friendly and they made me feel at home," he explains.

As soon as he converted into a central defender, the comparisons with the legendary Bobby Moore were inevitable. But Ferdinand, who made his senior debut on the final day of the 1995–96 season, grew up idolizing rather more exotic superstars – namely former West Germany skipper Franz Beckenbauer and Dutch ace Frank Rijkaard – both of whom he studied endlessly on videos.

In turn, Glenn Hoddle made a number of visits to Upton Park to watch Rio before calling him up, but it was his predecessor, Terry Venables, who gave the distant cousin of Les Ferdinand his first experience of international duty. When it arrived through the post, Ferdinand thought the letter inviting him to train with England's European Championship squad was a mistake. But once he reported to Bisham Abbey, he felt at home. "All the players made me feel like I was an England player and not just someone making up the numbers in training."

Settling in well

Almost 18 months later, he became the third youngest player to make his England debut this century, aged 19 years and eight days. It was a solid performance almost crowned by an assist for Robbie Fowler, whom he put through on goal, and it drew praise from Hoddle: "Rio got a little taste and he settled in well, which is promising for the future."

Although Ferdinand is unlikely to see much action in France – the England coach feels he needs more games to bed down – he has surely been earmarked for a sweeper's role in years to come.

In the meantime, the boy with the Brazilian name keeps dreaming. "I want to take West Ham to Wembley, I want a championship medal, I want 50 caps and I want to lead England." he says.

"If I could achieve half as much as Bobby Moore, it will have all been worth it."

Rio FERDINAND

Position: Centre-half
Place of birth: London
Date of birth: November 7, 1978
Height: 6ft 2in
Weight: 12st
Club: West Ham United
International debut: Cameroon (H), November 15, 1997
Appearances: 1
Goals: 0

Gareth **Southgate**

There must be better ways to celebrate the greatest moment of your international career.

While Glenn Hoddle and the rest of the England squad popped the cork in the dressing-room after the final whistle in Rome, Gareth Southgate and Teddy Sheringham were whisked off by FIFA officials for a drugs test. For the next two hours, the pair sat in a room with sombre-faced Italian duo Antonio Bennarivo and Demetrio Albertini, consuming vast quantities of water in an attempt to provide their all-important samples.

Nothing, however, could dampen Southgate's spirits after what was arguably his best performance in an England shirt. The year had started on a disappointing note when he was omitted from the team to face Italy at Wembley, and it took an outstanding display in the 2–0 win in Poland three months later to restore his poise and confidence. In between goals by Shearer

Gareth Southgate: had his share of highs and lows.

and Sheringham, a superb goal-line clearance by Southgate kept the Poles at bay.

"That game gave me a big lift," reveals the articulate and approachable Aston Villa defender. "I only got my chance because Tony Adams was injured, so it was an opportunity for me to stake a claim and win back my place. After an up-and-down season, I wanted to prove to people that I was still capable of playing at that level."

French leave

He did more than that. So impressive was his rehabilitation that he was the only player who started against Poland to keep his place for all three of the matches at Le Tournoi in France, where he tamed the impish Gianfranco Zola, snuffed out the French frontline and stood firm against the Brazilians.

And so to Rome, where a touch of Hoddle kidology had the journalists believing that Southgate would have to miss the game because of injury. Southgate did spend the final training session watching his team-mates from behind the goal, but only because he had already passed a fitness test and didn't want to aggravate an old injury.

At 6ft, he is the "smallest" of England's assorted centre-halves. But his speed of thought more than compensates for his relative lack of inches, and his versatility is one of his best attributes. He can operate in an orthodox back-four or as a deeper-lying sweeper at the heart of a 3-5-2 formation, epitomizing the modern, flexible system Glenn Hoddle has introduced among his squad.

"You need that extra depth and cover when defending against top-quality players," Southgate explains. "You can't gamble on the offside trap at this level and you need players who are quick.

"We've turned in some great performances in the last couple of years and shown that we can vary the line-up without dramatically affecting the performance. That sort of flexibility will be vital in a World Cup situation."

Gareth SOUTHGATE

Position: Centre-half
Place of birth: Watford
Date of birth: September 3, 1970
Height: 6ft
Weight: 12st 8lb
Clubs: Crystal Palace, Aston Villa
International debut: Portugal (H), December 12, 1995
Appearances: 22
Goals: 0

David **Batty**

It might come as a surprise to his dwindling band of critics, but until he was 28, David Batty had never been sent off in his life. So much for the hard-man image. Admittedly, he's been shown the red card three times since joining Newcastle United, but perhaps that says more about the recent crack-down in refereeing than it does about the stocky midfielder's game.

Either way, at international level Batty has been reborn under Glenn Hoddle. He made his debut as a 70th-minute substitute in a friendly against the USSR in 1991, but found himself in and out of Graham Taylor's teams, and spent a spell in the wilderness when Terry Venables was in charge.

Batty was recalled by Hoddle for England's World Cup qualifier against Georgia in November 1996 and has stayed in the frame ever since. He described his performance in the 2–0 win in Tbilisi as "my best for my country." Eleven months later, his display in the cauldron of Rome was arguably even better.

The Italian Job

Between them, Batty and Paul Ince subdued the threat of Italy's Demetrio Albertini and Dino Baggio, and it was the Yorkshireman who single-handedly held the fort while Ince was having his head wound stitched. After the match, Hoddle had nothing but praise for him: "Batty has been magnificent for 12 months. He isn't flamboyant, but he wins possession and rarely gives the ball away."

Batty claims that he would rather win a tackle than score a goal, adding that "midfield is the most important area in any game. If you win the midfield, you win – full stop."

But he is much more than just a "spoiler". Hoddle worked closely with him in training sessions during England's qualifying campaign, urging him to concentrate on playing the ball forward as quickly as possible after winning possession. As a result,

David Batty: under the watchful eye of Glenn Hoddle he's matured into a fine midfield player.

he has developed into a quick-witted, as well as sure-footed, force in midfield – another phase of the Hoddle masterplan successfully completed.

Batty is the only player in the squad to have won two Championship medals with different clubs – Leeds United and Blackburn Rovers – and his emergence as one of the country's finest midfielders has been overseen by an impressive list of club managers: Howard Wilkinson, Kevin Keegan and Kenny Dalglish.

He remains a quiet, unassuming family man who shies away from publicity and prefers to let his football do the talking. What's more, he is comfortable with the "squad game" philosophy which has become increasingly popular among the game's top coaches. Although he is very much a part of Hoddle's plans, he accepts that he may be left out of the side occasionally because his style does not suit a particular match.

It is hard to believe that he will not play a prominent role in England's quest for World Cup glory this summer.

David BATTY

Position: Midfielder
Place of birth: Leeds
Date of birth: December 2, 1968
Height: 5ft 8in
Weight: 12st
Clubs: Leeds United, Blackburn Rovers, Newcastle United
International debut: USSR (H), May 21, 1991
Appearances: 28
Goals: 0

Paul Ince

Paul Ince would like to set the record straight: he's neither England's "Guv'-nor", nor even Liverpool's "Guv'nor", and that's just the way he wants it to stay. He got the nickname at Manchester United, thanks to his habit of shouting "Who's the Guv'nor?" when he scored in training. It was a joke, he insists, which was blown out of all proportion.

It's just one more sign, like his new, improved brand of football, that Ince has come a long way since those halcyon days at Old Trafford, where his incredible success with United was occasionally blemished by a tendency to charge recklessly into tackles.

Paul Ince: bloodied but unbowed in Rome.

Don't dive in

"At United," Ince says, "I'd be flying in all the time and going to ground when I should have stayed on my feet. Playing in Italy taught me that you can't afford to dive in. It has also given me a better appreciation of what's going on, making me more aware of the situation around me."

Like so many England players on that October night in Rome, the Ilford-born midfielder had an inspired match – arguably his best in the white shirt – even though he spent part of it hurtling along corridors in the depths of the Stadio Olimpico. Ordered off by the referee to have stitches in a head wound, he dashed to the dressing-room only to find it was locked.

"I was shouting and screaming at all these geezers in Italian," he recalls. "In the end, the physio Gary Lewin had to go back to the dug-out to get the key." Eventually the skipper returned to the fray and resumed his perpetual-motion duties in midfield, repelling the home side and prompting his own troops forward. His bloodied head swathed in bandages, team-mate Paul Gascoigne later likened his inspirational skipper to a 'pint of Guinness'.

It was a performance which confirmed, if there was ever any doubt, just how crucial Ince is to England's World Cup hopes. He is, to quote coach Glenn Hoddle, "one of those players who feels he's an international footballer. He's got that inner self-assurance. Paul isn't as headstrong as he was, but he still wins the ball like taking sweets off a baby. If he could score goals as well, we'd have the complete footballer."

Admittedly, a tally of two goals in 34 internationals is a modest return, but Ince's strengths lie elsewhere, and there are enough talented individuals in the England side to take care of the scoring: names such as Shearer and Sheringham spring to mind.

Suffice to say that, in the heat of the World Cup battle in France, this is one footballer who will stand up and be counted.

But for goodness' sake, just don't call him you-know-what.

Paul INCE

Position: Midfielder
Place of birth: Ilford, Essex
Date of birth: October 21, 1967
Height: 5ft 10in
Weight: 12st 2lb
Clubs: West Ham United, Manchester United, Internazionale, Liverpool
International debut: Spain, September 9, 1992
Appearances: 36
Goals: 2

Robert **Lee**

Every international squad needs a player like Robert Lee.

A solid, consistent performer with a willingness to adapt and, occasionally, an eye for goal. Someone who will run until they drop, defending one minute, racing into goalscoring positions the next, and always prepared to cover for team-mates who are out of position. In short, someone you can depend upon.

At club level, the Newcastle United midfielder may not be as adventurous as he was under Kevin Keegan – he likened himself to David Platt during his attack-minded days – but he remains just as effective under Kenny Dalglish.

"Everybody likes scoring and I'm no different," he says. "I'm at my best going forward into the box and scoring goals. But sometimes it's not right for the team's build-up, and I think I've improved defensively."

Lee played twice in the qualifying campaign – at home to Georgia and away to Poland – and on both occasions his work-rate was outstanding. With the likes of Paul Gascoigne, Paul Ince, David Batty, David Beckham and Jamie Redknapp all vying for places in England's central midfield, he may struggle to make the starting eleven. But his versatility makes him a near certainty for the squad and he is still a big part of Glenn Hoddle's World Cup plans.

A goalscorer on his England debut

He won his first cap in October 1994, when he was 28 and scored against Romania into the bargain. But after a particularly exhausting season with Newcastle, he was left out of Terry Venables' squad for the 1995 Umbro Cup tournament.

"I wasn't playing well at all and the manager did me a favour, really," he confesses. "I was tired. It was the first year I'd played international football. You don't get a break. You train with England and play,

Robert LEE	
Position:	Midfielder
Place of birth:	West Ham
Date of birth:	February 1, 1966
Height:	5ft 10in
Weight:	11st 13lb
Clubs:	Charlton Athletic, Newcastle United
International debut:	Romania (H), October 12, 1994
Appearances:	15
Goals:	2

Robert Lee: a relative latecomer at international level, Robert Lee is now making up for lost time.

you go back to your club and there's another game on the Saturday and maybe one in midweek. It hit me. I was more relieved when I was left out. It gave me a chance to recharge my batteries. I would've done myself more harm than good."

Lee returned to England duty fitter and stronger than ever. A relative latecomer to international football, he has learned to be patient but is eager to make up for lost time.

"I want to win things, I want to play for my country," he declares. "The England thing has come late in my career and success, really, has come very late for me. When you're young, you've got other things on your mind, like going out and enjoying yourself, and when you lose you think, 'Yeah, so we lost.' As you get older, you appreciate it when the team wins every week. Now, I really don't want to lose, I want to win every game.

"I've got a medal for winning the First Division championship with Newcastle, and there's my England caps. That's it, really. Not much. There's a lot of space in my cabinet for silverware."

A World Cup winner's medal would do nicely, thank you very much.

David **Beckham**

The evening of February 12, 1997 was a grim one for Glenn Hoddle.

The rain had lashed down all day, England had just lost at home to Italy, and the hacks were in no mood for excuses. Amid the general gloom of the post-match press conference, one reporter asked the England coach whether David Beckham, who had played at wing-back against the Italians, might be considered for a central midfield role in the future. Hoddle was giving little away.

"I might give David the opportunity," he said. "But he's still got a lot to learn at this level."

Hoddle has never been one to stand in the way of youth. In his mind, four months was long enough. By June – and Le Tournoi – the Manchester United midfielder was ready to move into the thick of things. Once more, Italy were the opponents, but this time Beckham had the last laugh, demonstrating his precocious range of passing skills as England romped to a 2–0 win.

It was a watershed in his fledgling international career. Given the chance by Hoddle at the tender age of 22, he had proved that he could boss the midfield against one of the top sides in the world. In his third and most crucial match against Italy – the World Cup show-down in Rome – he reverted to a more conventional right-half position as England sought strength in numbers in midfield. Again, he hardly put a foot wrong.

As early as Beckham's first cap – in a World Cup qualifier in Moldova in September 1996 – Hoddle had predicted a glittering future for the lad from Leytonstone: "He's far more advanced than his age would suggest. He sees the furthest pass first. There are enough players around in English football who see no further than the nearest ball. If you can see the furthest, most penetrative one first, your options are so much more creative. David Beckham has got that ability."

Wonder goal

Three weeks before that Moldova game, Beckham scored a wonder goal from the halfway line against Wimbledon at Selhurst Park on the opening day of the season. Almost overnight, he moved into the superstar bracket. But he has always been a reluctant hero, describing himself as just "a young bloke enjoying his football and loving what he's doing."

David Beckham: the ball – and the world – is at the Londoner's feet.

A graduate of Bobby Charlton's Soccer School, Beckham made his debut for Manchester United's first team in 1995.

The 98 World Cup will be his greatest challenge yet, but he has the talent and maturity to rise to the occasion. Four years ago, almost no one had heard of David Beckham. This summer, his could be the name on everybody's lips.

David BECKHAM

Position: Midfielder
Place of birth: Leytonstone, London
Date of birth: May 2, 1975
Height: 6ft
Weight: 11st 2lb
Clubs: Manchester United
International debut: Moldova (A), September 1, 1996
Appearances: 12
Goals: 0

Paul **Gascoigne**

Ah, Gazza. Just how much water has flowed under the bridge since an outstanding display against Czechoslovakia at Wembley – he made three goals and scored a fourth – earned him a late call-up for Bobby Robson's World Cup squad in 1990? Eight incident-packed years on, his pace may have deserted him, but he remains England's talisman and his adrenalin-fuelled genius can still change a game in a split-second.

Whisper it, but Paul Gascoigne has matured, and just as well – his second World Cup brings new responsibilities. In Italy, he was the excitable pup, watched over by fellow Geordies Peter Beardsley and Chris Waddle. In France, he will be one of the oldest members of the squad – and he accepts that he must lead by example.

There were signs of this growing maturity in the titanic qualifier in Rome, where he curbed his natural attacking instincts in favour of a cool, disciplined performance on an otherwise frenzied night.

"We played the Italians at their own game," he said. "It was great to see them running after the ball. I knew I could keep the ball and pass it and make their players work a bit."

Credit must go to Glenn Hoddle for coaching – and coaxing – such unprecedented levels of control and concentration into the Rangers midfielder. Above all, Gascoigne has learned under Hoddle that there is a time and a place for adventure: as England's World Cup qualifying campaign gathered momentum, he stuck to his brief and began to kick his habit of losing possession in crucial areas.

Trust and loyalty

It is a relationship built on trust – something Gascoigne values highly. He turned down a move to the Premiership last year out of loyalty to Rangers manager Walter Smith. For his part, Hoddle stuck by Gascoigne at the height of the player's personal problems when the world must have seemed a very lonely place. The England coach has been repaid handsomely on the pitch.

Off it, Gascoigne remains unpredictable. He will always play the joker, but Bobby Robson, who experienced Gazza's effervescence first-hand back in 1990, wouldn't have it any other way. "If you take the daftness out of Paul Gascoigne you take away what

Paul GASCOIGNE	
Position:	Midfielder
Place of birth:	Gateshead
Date of birth:	May 27, 1967
Height:	5ft 10in
Weight:	12st 10lb
Clubs:	Newcastle United, Tottenham Hotspur, Lazio, Glasgow Rangers
International debut:	Denmark (H), September 14, 1988
Appearances:	54
Goals:	10

makes him special," he argued. "He just wouldn't be the same player."

For all his new-found temperance, Gascoigne's familiar forward bursts, mazy dribbling and sublime through-balls will be crucial to his country's progress in the finals. Prior to Euro 96, he had spent six years wondering where his next major tournament would come from. Injury robbed him of a shot at the 1992 European Championships in Sweden; two disastrous defeats deprived him of a summer holiday in the USA two years later.

At long last, he has the chance to bow out where he belongs – on the world stage as one of the game's greatest players. The clown prince has come of age.

Paul Gascoigne: has the player finally matured?

Steve **McManaman**

Steve McManaman: Is the best yet to come?

It's over eight years since the world – or more specifically 33,516 spectators inside Anfield – got its first glimpse of Steve McManaman.

On a grey, rainy December day in 1990, goals from John Barnes and Ian Rush gave league leaders Liverpool a 2–0 victory over bottom-placed Sheffield United. Ten minutes from the end, and with the game wrapped up, Peter Beardsley limped off to be replaced by a gangly teenager with a floppy fringe who made one promising run down the right wing which ended with a weak cross scuffed into the side-netting. Hardly the most spectacular debut for one of the most exciting players to grace the modern game.

McManaman should make a rather more significant impact in his first World Cup finals. The 26-year-old made a modest contribution to England's qualifying campaign, and there were even media rumours of a rift with Glenn Hoddle when the player pulled out of Le Tournoi last summer.

Nothing could be further from the truth. McManaman could no longer put off crucial treatment on his left knee, which he has dislocated three times during his short but scintillating career, and the England camp was kept fully informed of his progress.

For all that, the former teenage cross-country champion would be the first to admit that he has yet to repeat his club form at international level. "He's got immense talent, but he has yet to realize his full potential," says Hoddle. "There are things he needs to improve – basically, the end product."

A licence to thrill

But even though his role for England is more disciplined than that for his club, where manager Roy Evans has granted him a licence to thrill as a "floating" midfielder, it is surely only a matter of time before a moment of McManaman magic in the colours of his country confirms his credentials as a world-class act.

With each season in the Premiership, he matures with age and never fails to provide at least one contender for Goal of the Season. Who can forget the mesmerising run which led to his equalizer against Glasgow Celtic in the UEFA Cup, or his blistering goal at Newcastle in the Premiership?

Steve McMANAMAN	
Position:	Midfielder
Place of birth:	Liverpool
Date of birth:	February 11, 1972
Height:	6ft
Weight:	10st 6lb
Club:	Liverpool
International debut:	Nigeria (H), November 16, 1994
Appearances:	19
Goals:	0

McManaman is like his often injured teammate Darren Anderton in that his genius is often unpredictable . Although he could only secure a place on the bench towards the end of the national team's qualifying campaign, McManaman is sure to feature in France at some point. He gives Glenn Hoddle another option in midfield, an extra dimension to England's attacking play and has the potential to set the 1998 World Cup finals alight.

Expect the unexpected.

Jamie Redknapp: keep that stretcher away from me! – are his injury problems now behind him?

Jamie **Redknapp**

Halfway through last season, Jamie Redknapp fell to the ground clutching his ankle during a match against Newcastle United. The Liverpool bench was alarmed, BBC Radio Five Live commentator Alan Green feared the worst, and Glenn Hoddle, no doubt, held his breath.

Thankfully, no harm was done and the Liverpool player was able to continue after treatment. But it is a tribute to his undoubted ability and huge potential that the incident raised so much concern. Redknapp is held in high esteem by Hoddle, even though injury meant that he only featured in one game during the qualifying campaign – and that was on the bench.

In the course of winning eight caps, the luckless midfielder has been stretchered off no less than three times in England colours. Against Switzerland in November 1995, he tore a hamstring. In the memorable European Championship clash with Scotland in June 1996, he damaged ankle ligaments after coming on as a second-

Jamie **REDKNAPP**
Position: Midfielder
Place of birth: Barton-on-Sea, Essex
Date of birth: June 25, 1973
Height: 6ft
Weight: 12st 10lb
Clubs: Bournemouth, Liverpool
International debut: Colombia (H), September 6, 1995
Appearances: 8
Goals: 0

half substitute and transforming England's fortunes. Finally, in a friendly against South Africa last May, he broke his ankle and left the Old Trafford pitch knowing that he would miss Le Tournoi and England's remaining World Cup matches.

I'll be back

Ironically, it was also an injury which rescued his international career. Throughout the previous season, he had felt that he wasn't firing on all cylinders, and X-rays of the broken ankle revealed that a piece of bone had been floating around in the damaged area for the best part of the year.

"I haven't had much luck," he concedes. "It's funny, Gazza gets stretchered off like he's dead but manages to play the following week. I went to hospital for what I thought was a precautionary X-ray and ended up staying there for nine days! When I came off against South Africa, I felt sick and I began to think that people would start laughing at me. But I knew that I'd be back."

So did Hoddle. On the road to recovery, Redknapp, the son of West Ham boss Harry, was invited to train with the England squad. Hoddle has always had a soft spot for the 24-year-old playmaker – probably because so much of Redknapp's game reminds the England coach of himself.

Two years ago, Hoddle revealed that he might use Redknapp in a withdrawn role in front of England's defence, commenting, "He is such a good passer of the ball. He can hit a 60-yard pass or a 40-yard pass, but he sees the 60-yarder first. He's a better long-range passer than Paul Gascoigne."

Certainly, away from the frantic tussles of midfield, Redknapp's ball-playing skills would flourish in an area where he would have more time and space. Surprised by Hoddle's thoughts, Redknapp admits, "I'm always open to those sorts of things. My dad says that he can see me playing at the back."

Wherever he finds himself, he deserves a stroke of luck. After so many disappointments and false starts, the World Cup finals may just provide it.

Paul **Scholes**

England's first two goals in the friendly games at Le Tournoi in 1997 owed a lot to the French coaching supremo Gerard Houllier. That year, he lectured Hoddle and several other top English coaches about the art of getting the ball forward quickly, in particular scoring within ten seconds of winning possession.

England did just that against Italy in Montpellier. Paul Scholes picked up the ball inside his own half and played a 30-yard pass to Ian Wright, who surged away from his marker and scored. A series of rapid passes from Stuart Pearce to Wright to Scholes brought the second goal, dispatched with clinical efficiency.

Of course, the system will only work if you have the right players – and Scholes, architect of the first goal against Italy and executor of the second, is every inch the man for the job. In a match that he illuminated with his skill and confidence, it is easy to forget that this was also his first start for England.

Team-mate Stuart Pearce described it as the finest debut he had seen. Hoddle commented that Scholes "settled in effortlessly." In the nick of time – and to everyone's pleasant surprise – the Manchester United striker has staked a convincing claim for a place in the World Cup squad. In short, he has been a revelation.

Used to full houses

"When the boss first told me I was playing against Italy I felt nervous," he recalls. "But as soon as I thought about the game, I forgot it. I don't get nervous. Maybe it's because Old Trafford is always full, but I tend to feel confident in any situation. The goal was a bit of a surprise because I hit it with my left foot – but it's got to be one of my best. And it felt good at the end because there were half a team of us from Manchester United.

"I used to watch David Beckham and the Nevilles go off to join up with England, then sit down and

Paul SCHOLES	
Position: Striker	
Place of birth: Salford	
Date of birth: November 16, 1974	
Height: 5ft 7in	
Weight: 11st	
Clubs: Manchester United	
International debut: South Africa (H), May 24, 1997	
Appearances: 5	
Goals: 3	

Paul Scholes: the little goalscoring wizard scored his first for England against Italy in Le Tournoi.

watch the games as a fan – like I did when we played Italy at Wembley. I never felt bitter because they were there and I wasn't – but it does feel good to be a part of it now."

The Salford-born youngster, who grew up idolizing Bryan Robson, continued his sizzling international form with further classy goals against Moldova in the World Cup and Cameroon in a friendly. His development into a poacher supreme is all the more impressive in the light of a little-known asthmatic condition.

Without doubt, Scholes has a long and glittering international career ahead of him. The final word – for now – goes to Hoddle: "Paul is a superb finisher and he has a nice mentality and temperament. I'm delighted about the way things are going for him. He can play in three or four different positions, which is a major asset for any manager. On his debut against Italy, it was typical of him that he was almost embarrassed to be named Man of the Match."

Alan **Shearer**

January 17, 1998, was a red-letter day for Newcastle and England fans; Alan Shearer was back in action following his ankle injury five months earlier. Once he was out of plaster and back running and rehabilitating in the gym, Shearer's only major problem was boredom, and maybe a little envy as the likes of Robbie Fowler and Paul Scholes found the net for England. Not once, however, did his international absence worry him.

Alan SHEARER

Position: Striker
Place of birth: Newcastle
Date of birth: August 13, 1970
Height: 5ft 11in
Weight: 12st 6lb
Clubs: Southampton, Blackburn Rovers, Newcastle United
International debut: France (H), February 19, 1992
Appearances: 36
Goals: 16

"I don't see that my place is under threat," he shrugged. "How can it be when I'm not involved at the moment?"

After injuring his ankle in a pre-season tournament, Shearer spent 10 weeks in plaster. For almost six months, coach Glenn Hoddle was at pains to point out that England could live without the £15 million man – and the Shearer-less performances in the last two World Cup qualifying games proved it.

But Moldova, Poland and Georgia will testify that nobody does it better than Newcastle United's No. 9, who scored in every qualifier he played in apart from the first match against the Italians – when he wasn't fully match-fit. Without doubt, he is one of the most feared strikers not just in the Premiership, or Europe, but the world.

He's come back before

Aside from his goalscoring prowess, no one should underestimate Shearer's remarkable resilience. The ultimate professional, he has bounced back from injury before, notably the cruciate ligament rupture in 1992 which kept him out of the game for eight months while he was at Blackburn Rovers. He was arguably stronger when he returned and, of course, hungry for goals. So far, he has scored every 190 minutes of his professional career.

There have been other setbacks. As a teenager, he was overlooked by Newcastle and forced to leave his native North East for the other end of the country and an apprenticeship with Southampton. He responded by becoming the youngest player, at 17, to score a hat-trick on his full debut in the top flight. Arsenal were the hapless victims back in April 1988.

Since then, he has plundered defences and smashed records almost at will. Before his injury last year, he had scored by far the most Premiership goals (137), become the first player to score more than 30 Premiership goals in three successive seasons (31 in 1993–94, 34 in 1994–95 and 31 in 1995–96), and scored in a record-equalling seven successive matches for Newcastle between September and November in 1996.

All the more surprising, then, that his England place was reported to have been under threat prior to the 1996 European Championships. He ended his so-called goal drought in style, of course, scoring against Switzerland, Scotland, Holland and Germany to finish as the tournament's top scorer. Can he repeat the feat in France? If his phenomenal self-belief is anything to go by, the bookies should start lowering their odds now.

However England fare, the nations' favourite centre-forward is sure to make his mark.

Alan Shearer: England fans will be hoping to see their hero adopt this stance several times in France.

Teddy **Sheringham**

It began in The Den, south-east London, in the mid-80s. It will end – fingers crossed – in the Stade de France, north-west Paris, this July. If Teddy Sheringham does strike gold with England, there would be no finer way for his footballing odyssey to draw to a close.

If ever one player was responsible for the kind of fluent, thoughtful football that characterizes England under Glenn Hoddle, it is Manchester United's classy striker. The former Millwall, Nottingham Forest and Tottenham forward is a latecomer to international football, having made his debut at 27 in a World Cup qualifier against Poland in Katowice in 1993.

A 1–1 draw that night, followed by a shattering defeat by Norway in Oslo, all but ended his dream of playing in the 1994 finals in the USA. France, however, will find him at the peak of his powers and determined to make his mark.

If anything, Sheringham's contribution over the qualifying campaign has been underestimated, perhaps because, as a deeper-lying striker, he excels in touch and vision, rather than out-and-out goalscoring, although he still weighs in with his share – who could forget his two strikes against Holland in Euro 96?

Control freak

"From an early age," he explains, "all I ever wanted to do was score a better goal, control the ball a bit better, keep the ball up. It's amazing, but even today when I see players do things with the ball, I think, 'Yeah, I want to do that.'" His great passion is one-touch football – the kind that tore holes in Italy during the friendly between the two nations at Le Tournoi, France's World Cup warm-up, in the summer of 1997.

"We played some excellent stuff that day," he remembers. "I love to be involved in that. It's the best type of football."

At Manchester United, he acclimatized rapidly following his transfer last summer. Jürgen Klinsmann, no less, once described Sheringham as the best striking partner he had ever played with, and it is a mark of Teddy's progress over the last few years that it is so hard to imagine an England side without him. He was absent from the first three qualifiers – against Moldova, Poland and Italy – because of injury and it's no coincidence that they were also three of the team's less convincing performances *en route* to the finals.

Above all, Sheringham oozes confidence and self-belief. Listen to his tale about swapping shirts with Italian defender Alessandro Costacurta after England's 2–0 win at Le Tournoi:

"He looked at me with a wry smile and said, 'Now to Rome – very different.' I just looked back at him and said, 'Yeah, I'll see you in Rome. Love to.' He was trying to tell me, 'This means nothing,' and I was saying to him, 'I'm confident I can do it again.' I was happy with that little parting shot!"

The rest, as Signor Costacurta knows so well, is history.

Teddy SHERINGHAM

Position: Striker
Place of birth: Highams Park, London
Date of birth: April 2, 1966
Height: 6ft
Weight: 12st 5lb
Clubs: Millwall, Nottingham Forest, Tottenham Hotspur, Manchester United
International debut: Poland (A), May 29, 1993
Appearances: 30
Goals: 8

Teddy Sheringham: a goalscorer and goalmaker, his touch and vision will be vital to England in the World Cup finals.

Ian WRIGHT

Position: Striker
Place of birth: Woolwich, London
Date of birth: November 3, 1963
Height: 5ft 9in
Weight: 11st 8lb
Clubs: Crystal Palace, Arsenal
International debut: Cameroon (H), February 6, 1991
Appearances: 29
Goals: 9

Ian Wright: 'Wrighty' savours his goal against South Africa last summer.

Ian **Wright**

You're a proven Premiership goalscorer. You're called up for England duty by successive managers. But you end up on the bench so many times you get splinters.

What do you do? If your name's Ian Wright, you don't just sit there and sulk. You watch and learn. And who did you learn from? The master – Gary Lineker.

"Being a substitute so many times back then, I was able to watch Gary playing and that helped me a lot," reveals Wright. "I learned how to make the same runs."

Fast-forward to England's Le Tournoi match against Italy in France last summer. Paul Scholes receives the ball in his own half and looks up. Wright is level with Ciro Ferrara. Scholes plays an inch-perfect ball over the Italian's head. Wright takes the ball in his stride and lashes it home. Mr Lineker would have been proud of him.

"It's easy to do it if you've got the right midfielder to deliver good passes and a striker who is willing to run," adds Wright. "That's what my game is all about. No defender likes running towards his own goal, and if you're willing to do it all the time he'll lose concentration at some point, then it's up to you to finish."

Keep the faith

It was a goal – and a performance – which justified Glenn Hoddle's faith in a player who must have thought his England days were numbered. After scoring in a friendly against South Africa, the Arsenal forward was left out for the team to face Poland last May.

But patience is one of Wright's great virtues, and he returned with a vengeance, prompting Hoddle to comment, "You need people like him if you're going to be in each other's pockets for six weeks at a World Cup finals. I will remember that his effect on the other players has been brilliant."

Three months later, there were calls from some sections of the media for him to be dropped from the squad to face Moldova at Wembley after a final-whistle fracas with Leicester's Steve Walsh. But once again, Hoddle stood by his much-maligned striker. Typically, the first thing that Wright did when he arrived at Bisham Abbey was scrawl "I didn't do it" across a blackboard!

Wright's finest hour came in Rome. Deputizing for the injured Alan Shearer in the make-or-break final qualifying match, he ran himself into the ground for 90 minutes and almost scored at the death. He may not have scored, but it was arguably his finest performance in an England shirt.

For all that, there are no certainties in international football, and Wright knows that time is not on his side, especially with the likes of Andy Cole, Robbie Fowler and Michael Owen queuing up for a piece of World Cup action.

The chances are, he won't start England's first game in France, but his place in the squad is all but assured – by public demand.

Glenn Hoddle has experienced a roller-coaster ride during his short but sweet reign.

Chapter 4

The Coach

Ten years ago, Glenn Hoddle laid his cards firmly on the table. "For me, the ball is a diamond," he explained. "If you have a diamond, you don't get rid of it, you offer it."

Therein lies the philosophy which has transformed England into a team of world-beaters in the space of two short years.

England were already getting there under Terry Venables, but there was still plenty of work to do. In September 1997, on the eve of England's World Cup qualifier against Moldova at Wembley, Hoddle confessed that, "Taking over after the European Championships, I was on a bit of a sticky wicket. But I think I've got over that pretty well."

It was something of an understatement. By the end of 1997, his team had played 14 games, winning 11 of them and losing just twice. They had reached the finals of the World Cup, and just as importantly, they had done it in style.

"If I'd had any doubts I would not have taken the job," he admitted after the all-important goalless draw with Italy. "Terry Venables did a good job and that put more pressure on me when I decided to take over. But I've always believed that we have the right sort of players."

Glenn Hoddle has surrounded himself with coaching colleagues whom he knows he can trust.

Even so, they will only respond, of course, to the right sort of coach. There was never really any doubt. "Glenn has the charisma to carry the job," says Graeme Le Saux. "He was such a great player in his day that he instantly gains your respect, and that's all a coach needs to make a team respond."

As a player, Hoddle was destined for great things. "His touch on the ball was quite brilliant," recalls former England favourite, Trevor Brooking. "When I worked with him closely during England training sessions I saw him mesmerise team-mates with his skills."

Lifetime's ambition

Now, as a coach, winning the World Cup would be the culmination of a life's work. It has become Hoddle's single professional ambition. "Nothing else matters to me," he has declared more than once. To this end, he

has surrounded himself with like-minded assistants in John Gorman, Ray Clemence and Peter Taylor. Together, they have tackled a demanding, often frustrating job head-on and reaped the rewards. The result is a brave, new world in which England players combine their traditional virtues of grit and determination with continental technique. It's all about self-belief, and Glenn Hoddle has got it in buckets.

Every England footballer will vouch for Hoddle's exceptional ability, and none has a bad word to say about him. But perhaps the greatest compliment comes from his captain Paul Ince, who epitomises the drive and spirit in the current squad.

"Back in 1996, a lot of people said that Terry Venables should have stayed on as manager," Ince said. "But Glenn has taken us to a new dimension. We played four of our World Cup qualifiers away from home without even conceding a goal. That shows just how well he has prepared us."

(left) Hoddle the player won 53 caps for England, but his admirers say he should have won many more.

(right) A study in concentration, Hoddle watches his players perform from the dugout.

A new breed of coach

There's something special about Glenn Hoddle. He is the first of a new breed – an England coach barely out of his playing days – and he can communicate with his players. They understand each other, because 10 years ago he was sitting there, like them, looking up and listening to the boss.

"When I talk to them," he says, "they think, 'He sees it through our eyes, he's done it himself'. If they

can't see the picture, I'll try to paint it for them, but I don't show off. My day has gone. It's their turn now."

Widely regarded as the best two-footed player of his generation, Hoddle scored on his debut for England against Bulgaria in 1979. He played his last game against the USSR in the 1988 European Championship. After 53 caps, he was unceremoniously – some would say criminally – retired from international football at the age of 31. Neither Bobby Robson nor Ron Greenwood felt they could build a team around him, but many thought his considerable talents had been wasted. "Hoddle a luxury? It's the bad players who are a luxury," declared Tottenham legend Danny Blanchflower in 1981.

A year later, former Spurs manager Peter Shreeves was just as forthright in his views: "Brazil don't expect Zico to tackle back. It might be worth taking a chance on a midfielder whose principal asset is not his lungs."

Hoddle always harboured an ambition to return to

England duty – in the dug-out rather than the dressing-room. But it was not until he left Tottenham for Arsène Wenger's Monaco in 1987 that he was encouraged to follow his dream.

"My influence upon him may not have come from my coaching style," says Wenger, now in charge of Arsenal. "It was mainly that I tried to convince him that he could become an excellent manager. I had a feeling that he was not conscious of this fact, so I tried to show him that he could do it. Glenn has the qualities to do the England job very well. He has the determination, desire and intelligence and he should be given more time to prove himself. Football needs people like Glenn Hoddle."

Hoddle returned to England in 1991 and joined Swindon Town as a player-coach. Promotion to the top flight was secured with a thoughtful sweeper system – Hoddle was the spare man emerging from a central defence patrolled by two markers in Colin Calderwood and Kevin Horlock – which he was to refine with Chelsea, then England.

Upon his appointment at Chelsea, he vowed that he was, "single-minded and determined to bring success by playing the right sort of football".

A sweeping success

Little has changed since then, and the sweeper system is Hoddle's crowning achievement at international level. As early as his first game in charge, he was determined to make it work. Sure enough, in Moldova on September 1, 1996, his England team took to the field with David Seaman in goal, Gary Pallister, Stuart Pearce and Gareth Southgate in a flat back-three, Gary Neville and Andy Hinchcliffe as wing-backs, David Beckham, Paul Gascoigne and Paul Ince in midfield, and Alan Shearer and Nick Barmby in attack.

It was little short of radical, and it worked a treat. Since then, the names may have occasionally changed, but the system remains the same. It is not, however, set in stone. In Rome last October, Beckham and Graeme Le Saux were the wing-backs, but they were ready to switch to midfield and full-back respectively

Thanks to Hoddle's forward thinking, the foundations are already in place for his successor.

if the situation required a more orthodox 4–4–2 formation. Hoddle's predecessor Terry Venables was never keen on full-backs, claiming that it limited the number of chances to score. But to date, Hoddle's side have averaged 1.8 goals per game – a marginally better record than England under Venables.

The current England squad is the most versatile yet. Its players are comfortable on the ball almost anywhere and eager to assume new roles and responsibilities – and it's all part of Hoddle's grand blueprint for the English game. On the eve of the qualifier in Rome, the FA were drawing up a "Charter for Quality" under their technical director, Howard Wilkinson. Its aim? To improve the footballing education and coaching of the country's young players.

"There is a new respect for our football abroad," insists Hoddle. "To be fair to Terry Venables it started at the back-end of Euro 96, and we've been carrying on the good work ever since. If we do it the right way, good technique will be second nature to our players. It won't be achieved during my reign, but in 10 years' time the England manager will reap the benefits of what we are starting now."

This is an exciting time to lead England's finest into World Cup battle. But the future is bright, too. The future is Glenn Hoddle.

Life as an England manager

The faces may change, but the pressures remain the same. There have been nine England coaches since the war, and all of them have experienced their fair share of success and failure, praise and criticism. It can be the best job in the world, and the worst. National hero one week, public enemy the next, and more than a few grey hairs and sleepless nights along the way.

Even Hoddle has felt the wrath of England's more sensationalist press. After the defeat by Italy at Wembley, one tabloid newspaper announced that Hoddle "gave clear signs of losing the plot." His tactics, we were reliably informed, "indicated a lack of clarity and coherence in his thinking," while "his decisions invite the worrying question of whether the new England coach has yet grasped the difference between club and international".

Eight months later, of course, the same journalists were paying tribute to a coaching genius. England managers simply cannot win. A dozen years earlier, Bobby Robson told an assembled press corps, "If you people didn't exist my job would be twice as easy and twice as pleasurable!"

Hoddle knew exactly what he was letting himself in for when he accepted the post in 1996, and thankfully he has experienced nothing compared with the abuse suffered by some of his predecessors.

"You have to accept criticism as part of the job with England," admits Graham Taylor, whose four-year reign was marked by savage attacks in the newspapers. "But I think there is a difference between constructive criticism and personal criticism. I think all England managers, not just myself, have received too much personal criticism."

Vitriol in the media, however, is often the least of an England coach's worries. For a start, he has to impose his own personality and style upon his team, no matter how ruthless it may seem. When Bobby Robson named his first squad for a European Championship qualifier against Denmark in 1982, he dropped Kevin Keegan, who only learned about his omission through the newspapers. Keegan was naturally upset, but the same thing had happened to Robson on the eve of the 1962 World Cup finals when he was dropped in favour of an up-and-coming defender called Bobby Moore.

Winning players' support

At the same time, the coach must develop a strong relationship with his team while continuing to command respect. Alf Ramsey was fiercely loyal to his players, and Hoddle has shown support in times of crisis for the likes of Paul Gascoigne and Ian Wright, as well as encouraging them to play to their strengths and express themselves.

"He is the one England coach who has given me the confidence to do it at the top level," confides Wright. "In the past I've been asked to do things in the team that aren't natural to me. It's all a player can ask for – a bit of belief from the manager."

Motivation is only half the job. Not the least of Hoddle's achievements so far has been the introduction of the 3–5–2 formation and persuading his players to accept and embrace it. Footballers are not always open to new ideas, especially ones which differ from their style of play at club-level.

But Hoddle has won over his players and stamped his own identity upon England's football – some feat when you consider how infrequently the national team meets up and the prevailing attitude that continues to put club before country. As any former England coach would testify, after months of preparation there can be nothing more frustrating than a late withdrawal due to injury.

"When England are doing well in a major tournament, it can unite the country," argues Hoddle. "We must not lose sight of that fact. Chairmen and managers want their clubs to be successful, and rightly so. But I've never stopped an international player going to an international get-together, and that's because I have played for my country.

"Unfortunately, some people haven't played inter-

Faith can move mountains, and Hoddle is fiercely loyal to his England players.

national football. I know what it's like as a player to have limited periods of rest time. It's nothing new. We need fewer teams in the Premiership and First Division before the problem can be solved."

Mr Do-it-all

Gone are the days when an England coach had to organise everything from hotel bookings to travel arrangements for his squad. But he still has to combine the demanding duties of trainer, tactician and amateur psychologist – and all within the limited periods that the squad is together.

It is, according to Hoddle's predecessor Terry

Venables, "a crazy job. It's full of frustrations and the odds are loaded against you. But if you've got any competitiveness in you, you think there might just be a chance you can win… It's difficult, but not impossible."

Hoddle has proved that he has all the right qualities to succeed. In such a pressurized environment, failure is never more than 90 minutes away, but the rewards can be great. "In many ways it's more satisfying to reach the World Cup finals as a manager than a player," he reflects, "because I have to look after every single angle."

Past England managers

Prior to Glenn Hoddle, only half of England's eight previous coaches had guided England to the World Cup finals. The first was the bookish and bespectacled Walter Winterbottom, who took the national team to four consecutive tournaments between 1950 and 1962, all of which were dogged by poor organization and a general lack of interest on the part of his players and staff. Amazingly, England didn't take the World Cup seriously until the 1960s, and Winterbottom had no control over team selection.

"Each Football League chairman had his own personal list of who should play," he once recalled. "We used to discuss and discuss until we were down to, say, two goalkeepers and then a straight vote would decide."

As a result, a grand total of 34 players won just a single cap. A former RAF wing-commander and qualified PE teacher, Winterbottom spent 16 years combining his coaching duties with the role of FA Director of Coaching. He was also required to organize the team's travel and accommodation on tour and even cooked their food! When he resigned from the post, he moved on to the Central Council of Physical Education, where he was later knighted for services to sport.

World Cup winners

Winterbottom was succeeded by Alf Ramsey, a former England full-back who had managed unfashionable Ipswich Town to the Football League title in 1962. Upon his appointment, he declared that England would win the World Cup in 1966. But he lost his first match in charge – 5–2 to France in a European Championship qualifier – and his team failed to reach

Alf Ramsey was single-minded, determined and, not that he cared, not always popular with the Press.

the 1964 European Championship finals.

Ramsey, however, was determined and single-minded. At home on the training ground in his tracksuit, he insisted on picking the team without interference and instilled an "if selected" mentality among his internationals.

"In the past, England have been too reliant on players who later became injured or lost form," he said. "I want a squad, not a team, with players ready for first-team action when I call them."

In 1966, he masterminded England's finest hour by dispensing with wingers and introducing a revolutionary 4–4–2 formation. But four years later in Mexico, a combination of tactical mistakes and overcautiousness was blamed for England's exit in the quarter-finals. When his team failed to qualify for the 1974 finals, Ramsey was sacked. But his 73 per cent success record (played 113, won 69, lost 17) remains the best of any England coach.

There followed a bleak period in England's history. Don Revie replaced Ramsey but he defected to the United Arab Emirates midway through the ill-starred 1978 World Cup qualifying campaign.

Greenwood and Robson

His successor was former West Ham boss Ron Greenwood, who had qualified as a coach while still a player and groomed the likes of Martin Peters, Geoff Hurst and Bobby Moore at Upton Park. Inspired by the great Hungarian side of the 1950s and Brazil in the 1960s, he possessed a vast knowledge of international football and was the first English coach to champion the 4–2–4 formation.

"Football is a simple game," he explained. "The hard part is making it look simple." Initially, the 55-year-old accepted the post in a caretaker capacity, but he was an instant hit.

"He has got people believing in themselves and talking to each other," enthused England skipper Emlyn Hughes. "The family atmosphere had gone, but he's brought it back." Greenwood also unearthed some of England's finest post-war players, including Steve Coppell, Bryan Robson, Trevor Francis and a certain Glenn Hoddle. He led England to the 1982 World Cup finals in Spain and stood down when they narrowly failed to reach the semi-finals without losing a game.

Enter Bobby Robson, the second Ipswich manager to get the job in 19 years. The 49-year-old former England wing-half – he played in the 1958 World Cup finals – had won the FA Cup and UEFA Cup with the East Anglian club and coached the country's B team under Ron Greenwood.

Two years into the job, he presided over England's 2–0 victory over Brazil in a friendly in Rio, describing the wonderful solo goal by John Barnes as "one of the most important moments in my life." Although his England side failed to qualify for the 1984 European Championships, they arrived at the 1986 World Cup off the back of an 11-match unbeaten run.

Peter Beardsley partnered Gary Lineker up front and England made it to the last eight. Four years later, household names like Paul Gascoigne, David Platt and Gary Lineker helped the grey-haired Geordie to become the only England coach to reach the semi-finals on foreign soil.

He left England on a high to coach PSV Eindhoven, but his eight-year reign will always be remembered for the vicious campaign waged against him by the tabloids. It was nothing, however, to the treatment dished out to his replacement, Graham Taylor.

Bobby Robson enjoyed a good rapport with his squad but, like Ramsey, not with the newspapers.

Chapter 5
World Cup History

England's finest hour: skipper Bobby Moore is held aloft by team-mates after the epic 4–2 win over West Germany in the 1966 Final – 16 years after their first appearance in the World Cup.

Of the 15 final tournaments so far, England have featured in nine. They can be divided roughly into three eras: the trial and error of 1950, 1954, 1958 and 1962; the rise and fall of 1966 and 1970; and the renaissance of 1982, 1986 and 1990. The less said about the ones they missed – especially 1974, 1978 and 1994 – the better.

At the turn of the century, it was more a matter of finding teams to play than refusing them, and for the first 36 years of England's international history, the opposition was provided by the other Home Countries. The first match against Continental opposition came in 1908, when England travelled to Austria and won 6–1. It was a result which seemed to confirm their superiority over the rest of the world. That illusion lasted for another 21 years, until Spain beat England 4–3 in Madrid.

Yet still England refused to toe FIFA's line. They withdrew from the governing body in 1920, rejoined in 1924 and pulled out again in 1928 in a dispute over amateurism. In the early 1930s, France and Hungary punctured further holes in England's self-esteem. By the late 1940s, a run of good results, culminating in a 10–0 win over Portugal in Lisbon, seemed to suggest that England were back where they belonged – at the top of the pile.

But a nagging doubt remained: could England prove themselves in tournament conditions on foreign soil? More to the point, could they learn anything from countries like Uruguay and Italy, who had won the three World Cups held before World War Two?

In 1950, the answers were no and yes. England returned to the international fold with FIFA's blessing and made little impression in four consecutive final tournaments – despite boasting a legendary array of talent. Between 1950 and 1962 the national side won just three matches in final tournaments and were taught a lesson or two by superior teams. It was a

painful experience, but it served its purpose. In 1966, a new coach and a new team conquered the world. They may have won at Wembley, but England were champions on merit.

So where did it all go wrong? Perhaps England were guilty of developing a superiority complex after Alf Ramsey's achievements in the first third of his 12-year reign. Certainly, Don Revie's disastrous appointment and ultimate defection played its part. Either way, the 1970s were a bleak period in England's history.

Qualification for the 1982 finals marked the beginning of the road to recovery. A modest performance in Spain was followed by a place in the last eight in 1986, when they were undone by ungentlemanly conduct and genius in equal measure, and an epic tilt at reaching the Final four years later. As for 1994, let's just say that we've lived and learned from our mistakes.

On the eve of the finals in France, it's almost 50 years since England first took the World Cup plunge. It's been heroic. It's been heart-breaking. But it's never, ever been boring.

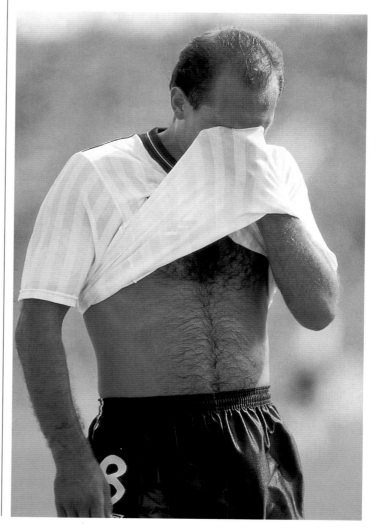

Midfielder Ray Wilkins is sent off during England's goalless draw with Morocco in 1986. Bobby Robson's team reached the quarter-finals.

Brazil **1950**

In the first half of the century, England made a habit of falling out with FIFA. But in 1946 they, along with Scotland, Wales and Northern Ireland, buried the hatchet and rejoined world football's governing body.

As a reward, the British Home International Championship was designated as a World Cup qualifying group, with the top two teams proceeding to the finals in Brazil. The Scots, however, insisted they would only go as British champions, and when England beat them 1–0 in front of 134,000 spectators at Hampden Park in April 1950, they decided to stay at home.

England, then, were Britain's sole representatives in a tournament which was dogged by disputes and withdrawals. Argentina, Czechoslovakia and France, among others, pulled out, leaving 13 countries. To complicate matters further, there were two groups of four, one of three, and one of two leading to the final 'pool' of four teams. In addition, a second-phase group competition was instated instead of straight and simple knock-out quarter- and semi-finals. Brazil played all their matches in Rio. The rest had to travel thousands of miles to fulfil their fixtures.

Nevertheless, England were installed as the pre-tournament favourites. In 19 games between September 1946 and April 1949, they had lost just once and scored 72 goals, and among the stars tipped to shine in Brazil were Tom Finney, Wilf Mannion, Stan Mortensen, Frank Swift, Stanley Matthews and Billy Wright. They also had a manager for the first time, but Walter Winterbottom's powers were limited.

To make matters worse, his preparations were disrupted by two unforeseen developments: the FA announced that a Select XI would embark on a goodwill tour of Canada during the World Cup and, simultaneously, Manchester United decided to tour the USA. Eventually, Winterbottom got the United players he wanted, but Matthews was contracted to appear in Canada. As it was, Winterbottom had his hands full cooking his squad's food in their Brazilian headquarters.

PEOPLE'S CHAMPION

Stanley Matthews

From England's point of view, there was little to cheer during the 1950 finals, but at least Stanley Matthews got his first taste of the World Cup. The "wizard of dribble" was English football's first superstar and a true crowd-pleaser, hugging the touchline and beating defenders with a trademark body swerve and an exciting burst of pace. The son of a professional boxer, he played for Stoke City and Blackpool, with whom he won the FA Cup in 1953, and made 54 appearances for his country over 22 years, the last coming at the grand old age of 42 in 1957.

Stanley Matthews was the hero of England's first finals in 1950, despite only playing one game.

Embarrassment

England found themselves in Pool Two with Chile, the USA and Spain. Goals by Mortensen and Mannion earned a 2–0 win over the Chileans in their first match, but what followed defied belief. Although the USA had lost narrowly to the FA's touring team in New York two weeks earlier, England hardly expected a contest.

Matthews had flown back in time to play, but the

selectors omitted him because they didn't want to change a winning team. The American part-timers, skippered by a Scotsman named Eddie McIlvenney, shocked their illustrious opponents with a first-half goal, and try as they might – they hit the woodwork five times – England could not find an equalizer. Back home, the result was greeted with total disbelief. "To be defeated by the United States at football was like the MCC being beaten by Germany at cricket," admitted Billy Wright.

England desperately needed to salvage some pride in their third match, but Spain were no pushovers. Jackie Milburn, brought in to bolster the attack, had a goal disallowed after 15 minutes, and the Spanish compounded their misery with a winning goal in the second half. England finished second in their group, and their first World Cup adventure was over.

In the second phase, Spain lost all three of their matches, finishing bottom of the group. As luck would have it, the championship was decided in the final match of the series between Brazil and Uruguay. Against all the odds, the Uruguayans triumphed in front of a record crowd of 199,854 in the newly-opened Maracana Stadium. The hosts went into the match needing a draw to become world champions, and they took the lead early in the second half. But a magnificent fightback by Uruguay saw winger Ghiggia set up an equalizer for Juan Alberto Schiaffino. Ten minutes from time, Ghiggia scored another goal after a fine solo run. Brazil laid siege to the visitors' goal, but Uruguay hung on to record their second World Cup success.

CLASSIC MATCH

USA 1 England 0

First round, June 29, 1950, Belo Horizonte.
Attendance: 10,151

After 38 minutes, a cross from Walter Bahr was headed home by Joe Gaetjens. England laid siege to the American goal, and Stan Mortensen and Jimmy Mullen missed easy chances. After his side's victory, US coach Chubby Lyons told reporters, "England congratulated us, though I knew how they must have felt. They showed the stiff upper lip which Hitler could never understand." It was a terrific shock to the system, but in time England would realize that they were no longer invincible and could learn a thing or two from the outside world.

Skipper Billy Wright leads England into action in 1950. The country's first appearance in the World Cup finals was instantly forgettable.

Switzerland 1954

Elimination in 1950 was a body blow and an embarrassment. England had travelled to Brazil as favourites to win the World Cup – they were so confident, they had arranged for their return flight from Rio to depart after the Final – but they returned with their tails firmly between their legs. It was time to pick up the pieces.

A 3–2 win over Austria in Vienna in 1952 went some way towards restoring morale. Then came one of the most historic matches in England's history. Hungary were something of an unknown quantity when they arrived in November 1953 for a friendly. When they went home, they were world-famous and they would not be forgotten in a hurry.

Orchestrated by Ferenc Puskas, the "Magic Magyars" systematically dismantled England's finest in an exhibition of football rarely matched since. It finished 6–3 at Wembley, and six months later it was 7–1 in Budapest. If there were ever any doubts about England's shortcomings on the international stage, they had been well and truly dispelled.

It was with some trepidation, then, that England prepared for the 1954 finals. Once more, they had qualified from a group consisting solely of Home Countries, winning their three matches with ease. This time Scotland, runners-up again, chose to join them in Switzerland. The English squad was experienced but perhaps a little old. The average age was 29 and Stanley Matthews, at 39, was back by popular demand. A lot rested upon the form of Nat Lofthouse, Bolton's battering ram of a centre-forward, and the ever-reliable Wolves defender Billy Wright.

Sixteen participants travelled to Switzerland, and the format of the competition was predictably confusing. Each country was to play just two first-round matches, even though the contestants had been divided into four pools of four. Two countries in each group were seeded to prevent them meeting in the first round, and the top two teams progressed to the quarter-finals. From then on, it became a straightforward knock-out tournament.

Ivan Broadis is challenged by a Uruguayan defender in the 1954 quarter-finals. England lost a game they could easily have won.

Sturdy centre-forward Nat Lofthouse pulls one back against Uruguay.

PEOPLE'S CHAMPION

Nat Lofthouse

Nat Lofthouse was brute strength in football boots. The son of a Bolton miner, he scored against Yugoslavia on his debut in 1951 and equalled Tom Finney's record of 30 goals for England seven years later. After a typically robust goal against Austria in 1952, he was dubbed "The Lion of Vienna" and voted Footballer of the Year twice on the trot. Ron Greenwood, later to become England coach, played against him at club level and recalled, "He used to make towering leaps at the far post and head the ball with tremendous power. He was very difficult to deal with."

Quarter-finalists

England were drawn in Pool Four with Belgium, Italy and Switzerland. Their first match – against the Belgians – was a cracker, the sides sharing eight goals in Basle. The hosts were next, and England dealt with them comfortably. A 2–0 win was secured with goals from the Wolves duo, Jimmy Mullen and Dennis Wilshaw, but the real talking point was Wright's successful switch to a more central role in defence.

Played two, won one, drawn one. Three points for England, two for Italy, and a place in the last eight for both.

CLASSIC MATCH

England 4 Belgium 4

First round, June 17, 1954, Basle.
Attendance: 14,000

One of the highest-scoring matches in England's history took place before a paltry crowd in Basle. The Belgians had beaten England just once in 13 attempts. But those previous encounters had produced 72 goals, so entertainment was always on the cards. England looked decidedly shaky at the back, but they still managed to go 3–1 up through Ivan Broadis (2) and Nat Lofthouse. Somehow, they let Belgium back in. After 90 minutes, it was 3–3, and extra time was played (another quirk of the tournament). Lofthouse scored his second goal, but another Belgian equalizer was inevitable.

Uruguay, twice winners of the World Cup and 7–0 victors over Scotland in the first round, provided the formidable opposition in the quarter-finals. It turned out to be one of the ties of the tournament, and one which England might have won if goalkeeper Gill Merrick had not made so many errors.

Early on, England went behind after a goalkeeping blunder, but Nat Lofthouse equalized on 16 minutes. Then Merrick misjudged a shot and England were behind again. Uruguay went three up before Tom Finney found the net an hour into the match. With England pressing for an equalizer, Merrick made another mistake and the South Americans scored their fourth. England had been bundled out of the competition again. At least they had progressed a little further, and this time they had not booked a late flight back home.

Perhaps it was a blessing in disguise – at least England had avoided the Hungarians, who proceeded to beat Uruguay 4–2 before losing to West Germany, a new force in world football, in the Final. Puskas had looked overweight, but he insisted on playing. The gamble seemed to have paid off when Hungary went two up inside eight minutes. But West Germany played a tactical blinder and were level midway through the first half. They sealed their triumph with a goal by Rahn and subsequently became the first unseeded side to win the competition.

Sweden **1958**

The four Home Countries were in different qualifying groups for 1958, and all qualified for the finals in Sweden. But it took a last-ditch equalizer to earn England a third successive crack at the World Cup. They had scored nine goals against Denmark in two qualifiers and beaten the Republic of Ireland 5–1 at Wembley. But a win over England in Dublin would put the Irish through. The home side led for most of the match, but it finished 1–1.

On paper, England were looking good. Between 1954 and 1958, they played 31 matches and lost only six times. In the process, they beat West Germany, the world champions, as well as Brazil and Hungary. But the Munich air disaster in February 1958 tore the heart out of the squad. In a terrible instant, Manchester United and England lost Roger Byrne, Tommy Taylor and Duncan Edwards, among others. All three had been destined for great things, and their deaths were sorely felt. One can only guess what they might have achieved for England in Sweden, let alone for United in Europe.

Walter Winterbottom drafted the largely unproven Johnny Haynes into his squad. He still had old hands like Stanley Matthews and Nat Lofthouse, but only four players in the party had played more than 10 times for their country, and there was no place for Brian Clough, who had scored 42 goals for Middlesbrough in the 1957–58 season.

England played the USSR twice in the 1958 finals. Here, Derek Kevan rushes in on Lev Yashin.

Costly lack of preparation

In time-honoured fashion, England's preparation was suspect, to say the least. Unbelievably, they arrived in Sweden just two days before the start of the tournament. They had not organized a training camp, and Winterbottom was left in charge of travel, accommodation and cooking. Once again – and quite literally – he had too much on his plate.

Austria, the brilliant Brazilians and the USSR, the reigning Olympic champions, provided England's opposition in Pool Four. To say it was a tough group was an understatement. The Soviets were first up, and their uncompromising tackling left its mark on the English and Tom Finney in particular. The Preston North End ace was injured within minutes of the kick-off but bravely continued. A good job, too.

The USSR scored two goals early in the second half but West Bromwich's Derek Kevan pulled one back and Finney dispatched an equalizer from the penalty spot with just six minutes on the clock. "Just when they should have been making the match an exhibition of scientific soccer, they turned it into a rough house," he recalled. "They tripped, they pushed, they kicked." Unfortunately, England hadn't seen the back of them.

In stark contrast, the subsequent match against Brazil, who had beaten Austria 3–0, was a treat for the purists. There were no goals, but either side could have won. England did themselves proud: they would be the only team to stop the eventual champions from scoring.

A rather less thrilling 2–2 draw with the Austrians a few days later was not enough to guarantee a place in the next round. England were on the same points as the USSR and a play-off between the two countries took place in Gothenburg's Ullevi Stadium. One goal won it, and it was scored by the Soviets. In a match bereft of accurate shooting, the most notable omission from England's team was Bobby Charlton.

They returned home to a cacophony of criticism from the Press. Attention had shifted to Wales, who had beaten Hungary in their own play-off to book a quarter-final tie against Brazil. It took a late, deflected effort from a 17-year-old called Pele – his first goal in the World Cup finals – to end Welsh resistance. Brazil met the host nation, Sweden, in the Final. Inspired by the scintillating skills of Didi, Vava and Garrincha, they won 5–2. It was the first – and so far, last – time that a South American country had won the tournament on European soil.

Billy Wright was a shining light to fellow professionals and a hero to millions of youngsters.

Chile **1962**

Football, like music and fashion, had succumbed to the spell of the Swinging Sixties in England. Kits changed dramatically, as did hairstyles, and – in 1961 – the maximum wage had been abolished. Footballers were becoming superstars in their own right. England duo Jimmy Greaves and Bobby Charlton were full-blown celebrities, and even lesser-known international team-mates like Bobby Robson and Jimmy Armfield were enjoying the good life.

At the start of the decade, it seemed the national team could do no wrong. Walter Winterbottom had gone back to the drawing board, copying Brazil's

Walter Winterbottom points the way ahead for England. He was coach for 16 years.

4–2–4 formation, and his side responded by scoring 45 goals in nine matches. England qualified for the World Cup finals without losing a game. Portugal and Luxembourg had stood in their way, and both countries were put to the sword, the latter losing 9–0 in their first qualifying encounter with the English.

If there was any worry, it was that England relied too much on Johnny Haynes, who had come of age as a striker – and the first footballer to earn £100 a week – with Fulham. But there was strength in depth in Winterbottom's squad, half of which had been capped 10 times or more.

Chile was an odd choice for the finals. Granted, the last two tournaments had been staged in Europe, but a host nation in South America with better stadiums and a tidier infrastructure had seemed more likely. For all that, England were delighted with their headquarters – a picturesque mining village 8,000 feet above sea level with a cinema, ten-pin bowling alley and golf course. For once, Winterbottom didn't have his work cut out.

Butchery overcomes artistry

The format of the competition was the same as 1958. England were drawn in Group Four with Argentina, Bulgaria and Hungary. From the start, it became apparent that this World Cup would be remembered for its butchery more than its artistry. The first-round games were dominated by over-physical contests and ugly scenes, particularly in the tie between Italy and Chile. Elsewhere, Pele limped out of the tournament following an injury against Czechoslovakia – sadly for him, the shape of things to come.

Argentina beat Bulgaria 1–0 in a dull opening to Group Four. The following day, England played Hungary, their arch nemesis, in the best game of the group. Haynes had a stinker, and it affected the entire team's performance. After 16 minutes, Lajos Tichy scored for Hungary. England weren't playing with any fluency, but they fought back well. Charlton hit the side netting with a pile-driver and Bobby Moore had a 30-yard effort turned over the bar. They were rewarded for their efforts after 58 minutes when Ron Flowers equalized with a penalty. But class prevailed 20 minutes from time when Albert scored a second for the Hungarians.

CLASSIC MATCH

England 3 Argentina 1

First round, June 2, 1962, Rancagua.
Attendance: 9,794

Games between England and Argentina have a habit of providing drama, and this match was no exception. The two countries had first met at Wembley in 1951, with England winning 2–1. Two years later, a match in Buenos Aires was abandoned after 23 minutes. The Argentinians had a fine World Cup pedigree, but they were outclassed in Rancagua by a team boasting the emerging talents of Bobby Charlton and Jimmy Greaves, both of whom scored after Flowers had given England the lead on 14 minutes. Argentina scored near the end, but it was mere consolation.

Ron Flowers, an unsung England hero, clears his lines against Italy.

England were a vast improvement against Argentina in their next match. They won 3–1, and their second goal was the first of many Charlton specials from outside the box. A 0–0 draw against the Bulgarians would see England through to the next stage as group runners-up. They got it – albeit to the jeers of a Chilean crowd who had come to see goals.

The quarter-finals pitched England against Brazil.

In three classic World Cup encounters, England have yet to get the better of the Brazilians, but neither have they been outclassed. This was the second meeting between the two countries, and England's hero was 21-year-old Moore, who was outstanding in the centre of defence. His team matched the world champions for an hour but eventually lost 3–1. Brazil winger Mario Zagallo, who would later become his country's coach, was complimentary: "England were a strong side. But we beat them as a unit."

Certainly, there was no shame in losing to the mighty men in yellow, who swept past Czechoslovakia in the Final. But an era in England's history had drawn to a close and changes had to be made. After 16 years as coach, Winterbottom resigned. Enter Alf Ramsey.

We are the champions! England parade the Jules Rimet trophy around an ecstatic Wembley Stadium after their enthralling encounter with West Germany which saw six goals.

CLASSIC MATCH

England 4 West Germany 2

Final, July 30, 1966, Wembley.
Attendance: 96,924

The manager: Alf Ramsey. **The team:** Gordon Banks (Leicester City); George Cohen (Fulham); Ray Wilson (Everton); Nobby Stiles (Manchester United); Jack Charlton (Leeds United); Bobby Moore (West Ham United); Alan Ball (Blackpool); Geoff Hurst (West Ham United); Bobby Charlton (Manchester United); Roger Hunt (Liverpool); Martin Peters (West Ham United). **The referee:** Gottfried Dienst (Switzerland). **The linesmen:** Tofik Bakhramov (USSR); Karol Galba (Czechoslovakia) **The goals:** Haller 13; Hurst 19; Peters 78; Weber 90; Hurst 100; Hurst 120. **The result:** 4–2 (after extra time). **The verdict:** the finest day in English sporting history. Need we say more?

England **1966**

As early as 1962, Alf Ramsey had predicted that England would win the World Cup. Four years later, the moment of truth had arrived. Ramsey was anything but a dreamer. He recognized that only a solid, efficient 4–4–2 outfit would stand a chance of becoming world champions, and to this end he picked players who were loyal, hard-working and patient, among them new faces like Geoff Hurst, Martin Peters, Alan Ball and Nobby Stiles. The backbone of the team remained the same: Gordon Banks, Bobby Moore and Bobby Charlton.

England had been drawn in Group One with France, Mexico and Uruguay. The coach had let his players return to their homes before re-assembling three days before the opening game. They were relaxed when they ran out at Wembley Stadium, but neither Roger Hunt nor Jimmy Greaves, the two main strikers, could break down a rigid Uruguayan defence, and a goalless draw did little to suggest that Ramsey's prophecy would come true.

A dramatic improvement was needed, and it came against Mexico. A Bobby Charlton pile-driver opened England's account seven minutes from half-time, and in the second half Hunt scored after a shot by Greaves had been saved. In England's final group match, Ramsey fielded a team without any recognized wingers. France had to win by four clear goals to progress, but Hunt scored a goal either side of half-time to end their interest in the competition. The biggest shock in the other groups was Italy's elimination after a demoralizing defeat by North Korea. The Brazilians, too, were out. They had lost to Hungary and Portugal, and Pele had been kicked from pillar to post.

Argentina, though, were still there, and their quarter-final showdown with England is not remembered for the quality of the football. Shortly before half-time, Argentina skipper Antonio Rattin was sent off. It took him 10 minutes to leave the pitch. The deadlock was broken in the final 15 minutes when a cross from Peters was headed home by his West Ham team-mate Hurst, who had replaced the injured Greaves. After the match Ramsey warned, "We have still to produce our best football. It will come against a team who come to play football and not act as animals."

The semi-final against Portugal, who were competing in their first World Cup finals, was a huge contrast. No foul was committed until the 23rd minute. Two goals by Bobby Charlton proved decisive. Stiles shackled Eusebio, the tournament's top scorer, until the final five minutes, when the striker converted a penalty. The other semi-final was a dull affair won by West Germany over the USSR.

Final glory

On a greasy pitch, Helmut Haller opened the scoring in the first 15 minutes, but Hurst equalized soon after, heading home a Moore free-kick which the two players had worked on frequently at West Ham, but not for England.

Peters gave England the lead with 12 minutes remaining, but it was cancelled out by Wolfgang Weber in stoppage time. There was barely time to restart before the final whistle went. As the players sat down, Ramsey uttered his famous pep talk. "You've beaten them once. Now go out and beat them again."

Ten minutes into the extra period, Ball dashed to the touchline, crossed, and Hurst hooked his shot against the underside of the bar. Everyone on the England bench leapt to their feet – except Ramsey – and Hunt, following up like the predatory striker he was, wheeled away without bothering to net the rebound, certain it was a goal. The referee was unsure and went over to his Soviet linesman, Mr Bakhramov, before pointing to the centre circle.

When Hurst completed his hat-trick in the dying seconds, and the final whistle was blown, everyone on the bench jumped for joy – except Ramsey. He remained calm, but he was the happiest man inside Wembley. He said they would win it, and they had. *The Sunday Times* declared, "The England team's triumph is inseparable from his own."

PEOPLE'S CHAMPION

Nobby Stiles

He may not have been the world's most gifted player, but Norbert Peter Stiles was never short on guts. His finest performance for England came in the semi-final against Portugal, when he man-marked Eusebio for 90 minutes. "I couldn't let Eusebio set himself to score because he didn't need much room for a shot," he recalled. "His foot was like a trigger, so I had to keep him unbalanced. If you are marking a great player, you have to keep chasing him. If everyone else is having a great and entertaining match, you have to resist the temptation to join in."

Nobby Stiles pays close attention to Eusebio during England's semi-final against Portugal.

Mexico **1970**

As reigning world champions, England qualified automatically for the finals. The previous year they had undertaken a tour of Central and South America to acclimatize to the conditions in Mexico, and there were signs on that trip of the problems which would plague the England camp in 1970. Alf Ramsey was awkward and aloof with the Mexican press, and back home he came under increasing attack for his negative tactics.

His squad, however, was formidable. It boasted experience from the likes of Bobby Moore, Gordon Banks and Bobby Charlton, and there were new additions in the shape of Francis Lee, Colin Bell, Jeff Astle, Norman Hunter, Alan Mullery, Allan Clarke and Terry Cooper. "We all felt that we were probably the strongest squad England had ever had in their history, stronger even than in 1966," claimed Mullery. "We were convinced that we could win it."

They could not have foreseen the bad luck which struck before their arrival. Skipper Bobby Moore was arrested in Bogota on charges of theft and spent four days in a Colombian prison cell. When the party finally touched down in Mexico, striker Jeff Astle, a nervous flyer, was the worse for drink and one Mexican newspaper described England as a "team of thieves and drunks." If anything, the English made it worse by importing their own food.

Ramsey's men were anxious to get on the pitch and prove their mettle. They had been drawn in a tough group in Guadalajara and their opening match against Romania was marred by rough-house tactics from the East Europeans. Blackburn's Keith Newton, a talented full-back, limped off after a tackle by Mocanu, and substitute Tommy Wright received similar treatment.

CLASSIC MATCH

Brazil 1 England 0

First round, June 7, 1970, Guadalajara.
Attendance: 66,000

The clash of the titans, played out in the blistering midday heat of Guadalajara and remembered for Brazil's all-star cast – Pele, Jairzinho, Rivelino, Tostao, Gerson, Carlos Alberto – and England's heroic performance. Ramsey's team had been kept awake all night by noisy fans outside their hotel, and it showed. After 10 minutes, Gordon Banks somehow turned Pele's goalbound header around the post. On the hour, Jairzinho fired home from a neat Pele assist. Alan Ball hit the crossbar, Jeff Astle missed a sitter, and Brazil clung on. Famously, Bobby Moore swapped shirts with Pele on the final whistle.

Hurst got the only goal of the game, shooting through the goalkeeper's legs after 65 minutes.

Brazil crushed Czechoslovakia 4–1 in another Group Three match, and four days later the samba kings met the world champions in a match billed as the unofficial final. It was an unforgettable encounter, and only a goal by Brazilian winger Jairzinho separated the two teams after 90 minutes. It was a set-back for England, but they ensured their place in the second round by beating the Czechs 1–0 with a second-half penalty from Clarke.

Holders go out

The quarter-finals pitched them against West Germany in Leon – the first meeting between the two countries since 1968. England seemed to have the edge, having lost to the Germans just once in nine previous matches. But they were cursed by more bad luck

A fantastic match, a fantastic photograph. Pele and Moore swap shirts in Mexico.

Geoff Hurst, hat-trick hero in 1966, goes close against Brazil four years later.

and some tactical naiveté.

Hours before kick-off, Banks was taken ill with food poisoning and Peter Bonetti was drafted in between the posts. England raced ahead with glorious goals from Mullery and Peters before casually, fatally, taking their foot off the gas. England had never thrown away a two-goal lead, but they were far too complacent.

No sooner had Franz Beckenbauer's weak shot crept past Bonetti after 68 minutes than Ramsey decided to take off Bobby Charlton and rest him for the semi-finals. It was Charlton's 106th and – it turned out – last international. "To see the back of Bobby Charlton was a great psychological boost for us," claimed Beckenbauer after the match.

On came Colin Bell, followed by Norman Hunter for Martin Peters. By now, German substitute Jürgen Grabowski was running rings around exhausted full-back Terry Cooper and gaps were beginning to appear in the English defence. With ten minutes remaining, Uwe Seeler beat the offside trap to loop a header over

PEOPLE'S CHAMPION

Geoff Hurst

Geoff Hurst's career is inextricably linked with West Germany. The prolific West Ham striker made his debut against the Germans in a friendly in February 1966, scored the only hat-trick in a World Cup final against them four months later, and won his last cap against the same opposition in 1972. Overall, he scored 24 goals in 49 internationals and averaged a goal every two games for his club. By 1970, he was firmly established as a national hero. Although he only scored one goal in Mexico, his tireless running and bravery in the box were essential to England's cause.

Bonetti, and in extra-time Gerd Müller capped an astonishing comeback with a close-range volley. England had engineered their own downfall, but they had made another magnificent contribution to the World Cup and left with Pele's praises ringing in their ears.

"The English team have some outstanding players," he declared. "Men like Banks and Moore and Bobby Charlton. They can take on any Brazilian team at any time – and that is no light compliment."

Spain **1982**

"We're on our way, we are Ron's twenty-two, hear the roar of the red, white and blue…" So began the song which accompanied England to the 1982 World Cup finals. Fate, however, had already conspired against them. They arrived in Spain with key men injured, and they returned unbeaten but eliminated.

Ron Greenwood, selected as manager ahead of Brian Clough, Lawrie McMenemy and Bobby Robson, had been close to resigning after England's win over Hungary in a vital qualifier a few months before the finals. But on the flight home from Budapest, he was talked out of it by Kevin Keegan and Trevor Brooking.

As it was, England arrived in Bilbao with a modest record in the qualifying campaign but an improve-ment in recent form. They had lost three of their qual-ifiers in an average group, but five wins and a draw in their World Cup warm-up matches provided grounds for optimism. Awaiting them in Group Four were France, Czechoslovakia and Kuwait.

Greenwood had built a team around stars from Manchester United and Ipswich. In midfield, he relied on the Old Trafford trio of Ray Wilkins, Bryan Robson and Steve Coppell, with Arsenal's Graham Rix replac-ing the injured Brooking. The East Anglian club was represented by Terry Butcher, partnering Liverpool's Phil Thompson in central defence, skipper Mick Mills at right-back and striker Paul Mariner alongside Trevor Francis in attack. Another notable absentee was Kevin Keegan, troubled by a back injury, and there was no place in the squad for wingers Laurie Cunningham and Peter Barnes.

Bryan Robson scores one of the fastest goals in World Cup history. France are on the receiving end.

Ron Greenwood: a popular choice as coach.

Fastest finals goal

Any doubts about the strength of Greenwood's squad were dispelled within half-a-minute of the opening match against France, when Bryan Robson scored the first of two goals in a comfortable 3–1 win. Greenwood named the same side for the game against the Czechs – the first time he had fielded an unchanged team in 33 internationals.

Czechoslovakia, who had been held to a draw by Kuwait, kept England at bay for an hour before Francis scored from a Wilkins cross. Three minutes

CLASSIC MATCH

England 3 France 1

First round, June 16, 1982, Bilbao.
Attendance: 44,172

Just 27 seconds of this eagerly anticipated encounter had passed when Bryan Robson scored one of the fastest goals in the history of the World Cup. A throw-in from Steve Coppell was headed on by Terry Butcher and Robson lashed the ball home from close range – the perfect start. The much-fancied French drew level through Soler on 25 minutes, but England refused to panic and Robson restored their lead with a header midway through the second half. With eight minutes left, Paul Mariner wrapped it up after a Trevor Francis shot bounced off a defender's legs.

PEOPLE'S CHAMPION

Ray Wilkins

Raymond Colin Wilkins was 25 and at the peak of his powers during the 1982 World Cup finals. England's elegant driving force in midfield made his debut against Italy aged 19, and went on to win 84 caps for his country over 10 years. His critics pointed out that he scored just three goals for England and made too many square passes, but teammate Trevor Brooking spoke for the majority when he described the Manchester United man as "a wonderful player with a big-match temperament and the ability to hit passes that few other players in the world could surpass."

later, Czech defender Barmos deflected a ball from Mariner into his own net, and England had recorded their eighth win in nine matches.

Kuwait, who had lost heavily to the French, proved the most difficult side to break down. Francis scored the only goal of a dreary match, and England joined Brazil as the only other team to qualify for the next stage with maximum points.

There was a new format for the second stage, with four groups of three countries and a place in the semi-finals for group winners at stake. England were joined by reigning European champions West Germany and Spain in Group B. The Germans had beaten England four times in their last six meetings and were clear favourites to reach the last four. Pundits were predicting another classic encounter, but the match in Madrid fizzled out into a goalless draw, with both sides lacking punch up front. Robson had a fine header saved by Harald Schumacher in the first half, and Karl-Heinz Rummenigge shook Peter Shilton's crossbar with a fierce shot three minutes from time.

Because West Germany had beaten Spain 2–1, it meant that England had to beat the hosts by two clear goals – or by one goal if they scored three or more – to reach the semi-finals. If they won 2–1, they would be on the same points as the Germans, and lots would have to be drawn; a 1–0 defeat would mean elimination.

Keegan, the man who could make all the difference, flew to Hamburg for specialist treatment on his back injury. Half-an-hour from the end of the game, and with the game goalless, he came on and missed a point-blank header. "There are no excuses," he admitted after the match. "I should have buried it."

England had 24 shots on goal to Spain's two. They had won three games, drawn two and conceded just one goal. But they were out. "Being given chances and taking them," sighed Greenwood. "That's what life is all about."

Mexico 1986

Four years into his spell as coach, Bobby Robson was at the centre of an unprecedented hate campaign launched by the Press. In the build-up to the 1986 finals, one journalist wrote that "his natural expression is that of a man who fears he might have left the gas on."

The slurs were all the more inexplicable because England had arrived in Mexico off the back of an 11-match unbeaten run. They had won four and drawn four of their qualifying games, scoring 21 goals and conceding just two, and in Gary Lineker they had a world-class marksman who had scored 30 goals for Everton during the domestic season.

England's first match, however, was a nightmare. In the 100-degree heat and humidity of Monterrey, a town on the border with the USA, they wilted against Portugal. Fourteen minutes from the end of a dull game, a mistake by full-back Kenny Sansom allowed Carlos Manuel to score. Lineker, who had sprained his

PEOPLE'S CHAMPION

Peter Beardsley

Gary Lineker grabbed the goals in Mexico, but he owed plenty to Peter Beardsley, whose gap-toothed grin will live long in the memory. The diminutive Geordie had made his England debut in a 4–0 win over Egypt in January 1986, but he was denied a starting place in the finals by Mark Hateley, an old-fashioned centre-forward. When Bobby Robson realised that Lineker needed a more cunning partner up front, Beardsley got the nod and he responded with arguably his finest performance in an England shirt against Poland in Monterrey. He returned a hero and eventually notched up over 50 caps.

Goals from Lineker and Beardsley against Paraguay secure a place in the 1986 quarter-final.

wrist during a friendly against Canada ten days earlier, failed to develop an understanding with his partner Mark Hateley, and when Bryan Robson was substituted with what turned out to be a dislocated shoulder, England lost their rhythm entirely.

It was the worst possible start, and the situation hardly improved in the next match against Morocco. Just before half-time, Robson dislocated his shoulder again and trudged out of the tournament. Within a minute, acting skipper Ray Wilkins threw the ball away in frustration after an offside decision and was sent off by referee Gabriel Gonzalez. He became the first Englishman to be dismissed in the World Cup finals and received a two-match suspension. The ten men held out for a point, but their immediate future in Mexico looked bleak.

On the eve of the final group game against Poland, Bobby Robson gathered his squad together and discussed their tactical options. Changes were made, and they worked a treat. England ran out 3–0 winners – all the goals coming from Lineker – against a team which had reached the last four in 1982. Robson's new-look side qualified behind Morocco, who became the first African team to reach the second round.

Unfancied Paraguay stood between England and a place in the last eight. After a cagey first half, the South Americans were summarily dispatched with two goals from Lineker and a third from Peter Beardsley, who had replaced Hateley as England's second striker. The match was played in Mexico City – a smoggy but pleasant change from Monterrey, where the players had lost up to a stone in weight during matches and experienced breathing difficulties.

"The Hand of God"

The quarter-finals had neutrals rubbing their hands with anticipation: England were to face Argentina for the first time since the Falklands conflict. In the magnificent Azteca Stadium, two very different goals by Diego Maradona gave Argentina a seemingly unassailable lead in the second half.

The first was blatantly punched into the net. "I knew what had happened straight away," claimed England goalkeeper Peter Shilton. "But the linesman looked at me and just ran off up the touchline." Maradona's second goal was legitimate and breathtaking. He picked the ball up near the halfway line, left four England players in his wake and slid the ball past Shilton.

After a defeat and a draw, England burst into life in their third game in 1986 against Poland. Gary Lineker scored all three goals without reply.

CLASSIC MATCH

England 3 Poland 0

First round, June 11, 1986, Monterrey.
Attendance: 22,700

It was the game England had to win, and they did so in style. Bobby Robson switched from a 4–3–3 formation to 4–4–2 and made the necessary changes. He drafted in Steve Hodge and Peter Reid for injured Bryan Robson and suspended Ray Wilkins, and replaced Mark Hateley and Chris Waddle with Peter Beardsley and Trevor Steven. The new team took the first half by the scruff of the neck and were three up inside 35 minutes. Lineker scored them all to notch the first hat-trick in the finals since Geoff Hurst in 1966.

Desperate times called for desperate measures, and Bobby Robson played his last card – John Barnes. The Watford winger came on for Trevor Steven and tormented the Argentinian defence. With nine minutes left, his cross was met by Lineker's head – his sixth goal of the tournament – and England had a lifeline. Three minutes from time, an identical cross from Barnes seemed destined for Lineker again, but this time it was intercepted by a defender. Argentina hung on, and England went out.

(Overleaf) Rival skippers Diego Maradona and Peter Shilton shake hands before the controversial 1986 quarter-final between England and Argentina, which England eventually lost.

Italy **1990**

England began the tournament dismally but, in the end, were desperately unlucky not to reach the Final. Paul Gascoigne came of age, David Platt came to prominence, and Peter Shilton carved out a niche in World Cup history. Chris Waddle, Stuart Pearce, Des Walker, Peter Beardsley and Gary Lineker were at the peak of their powers. For Shilton and Terry Butcher it was an unforgettable swansong.

On the eve of the finals, manager Bobby Robson announced that he would be joining PSV Eindhoven after the tournament. He had endured more than his fair share of pressure – with plenty of grey hairs to prove it – but he remained popular among his squad. Chris Waddle later recalled, "Bobby was loyal to his players and had bags of enthusiasm. He wanted us to enjoy our football, but he could never remember our names!"

England and their fans were based in Sardinia for the first round. They had been drawn against the Republic of Ireland, Holland and Egypt. The Irish provided the first test, and the direct football of Jack Charlton's side knocked England out of their stride. Lineker put England ahead after eight minutes, but they were pegged back in the 68th minute when Kevin Sheedy robbed Steve McMahon on the edge of the box and fired home.

It could only get better for England, and it did. They salvaged their pride with a magnificent performance in a goalless draw with Holland. Robson's players persuaded him to introduce a sweeper system at the back. Mark Wright was recalled for the first time since 1988, and his partnership with Butcher and Walker nullified the threat of Marco van Basten and Ruud Gullit. In the last minute, England thought

David Platt scored three goals in the 1990 finals in Italy – against Belgium, Cameroon and the hosts.

they'd won when Pearce drove a free-kick past Dutch goalkeeper Hans van Breukelen, but the referee ruled that the kick had been indirect. Five days later, a 1–0 victory over a negative Egyptian side – courtesy of a late Wright header – put England on top of Group F.

Penalty deciders

Their opponents in the second round were Belgium, who provided a stern test. Inspired by midfielder Enzo Scifo, they hit the post twice and kept England out until the last minute of extra time, when a free kick from Gascoigne was dramatically volleyed home by substitute David Platt. England had reached the quarter-finals for the sixth time in their history.

Waiting for them were Cameroon, who had beaten Argentina in the opening match of the tournament. It took 120 minutes to settle an enthralling contest in Naples, but a pair of Lineker penalties eventually earned England a 3–2 victory and set up a mouth-watering semi-final against West Germany.

The Germans had cruised into the last four with impressive wins over Yugoslavia and Holland, but Robson's improving side had the better of the first half. After 59 minutes, they went behind to a deflected Andreas Brehme free-kick. With ten minutes on the clock, Lineker converted a Paul Parker cross to force extra time.

Waddle and Guido Buchwald hit the post in the extra period, but the sides remained level. Gascoigne had been booked for a challenge on Thomas Berthold. Aware that he would miss the final if England won, he burst into tears. In the subsequent penalty shoot-out, successful spot-kicks by Lineker, Beardsley and Platt were matched by the Germans before Pearce's effort

England and Belgium take to the field in the second round. It took a goal in the last minute of added time to separate them.

PEOPLE'S CHAMPION

Terry Butcher

At 6ft 4in and weighing 14 stone, Terry Butcher was a formidable figure in the heart of England's defence. The left-footed centre-half played in three consecutive World Cup tournaments, retiring after the semi-final defeat by West Germany in 1990, and is the country's 10th most capped player with 77 appearances. He missed the 1988 European Championships with a broken leg but became a firm favourite with the fans after his performance in the goalless World Cup qualifier against Sweden in 1989, when he battled on with 10 stitches in a head wound. England lost just 10 times when he played.

was saved by the goalkeeper and Waddle blazed over. So near and yet so far.

"No team deserved to win because no team deserved to lose," said German coach Franz Beckenbauer.

A third-place play-off against Italy was scant consolation, but England held their own against the host nation, with David Platt equalizing Salvatore "Toto" Schillaci's goal before the Italian converted a late penalty. Peter Shilton made a record 125th international appearance, and both he and Bobby Robson bowed out in style. England had failed to win the World Cup, but they had won a new army of admirers.

CLASSIC MATCH

England 3 Cameroon 2

Quarter-final, July 1, 1990, Naples.
Attendance: 55,205

England kept their cool to overcome the Africans in a heart-stopping match. David Platt headed England into the lead after 25 minutes, but 38-year-old substitute Roger Milla set up goals for Emmanuel Kunde and Eugene Ebwelle in the second half. With seven minutes remaining, Gascoigne fed Lineker, who was tripped by Benjamin Massing in the box. Lineker converted the spot-kick and repeated the feat in extra time after goalkeeper Thomas N'kono had fouled him. "We pulled it out of the fire," admitted Bobby Robson. "At one time I thought we were on the plane home."

Missed **World Cups**

Did he not like that? England coach Graham Taylor is restrained during the defeat by Holland which effectively eliminated his team from the 1994 qualifiers – a campaign to forget.

England have been absent from six finals tournaments, half because they were ineligible – not being members of FIFA – and half because they failed to qualify. It's difficult to gauge how they would have fared in those first three competitions.

In 1929 England were beaten by non-UK opposition for the first time in their history – Spain were the victors in Madrid – and in the subsequent decade they lost to Czechoslovakia, Austria, Belgium, Switzerland and Yugoslavia, as well as Scotland and Wales. However, in 1934, they beat Italy, the reigning world champions, and four years later they crushed Germany 6–3 in Berlin.

Either way, the insular English would not have enjoyed the trip to Uruguay in 1930. Holland, Spain, Italy and Sweden all withdrew when their bids to host the tournament were rejected in favour of Uruguay, who were awarded the competition on the proviso that they built a new, 100,000-capacity stadium and paid the expenses of all the participants.

Eventually, four teams made the three-week voyage via steamboat from Europe to compete with another nine teams from the Americas. In the final, the hosts put four past Argentina with one-armed striker

Hector Castro scoring the final goal. While a national holiday was proclaimed in Uruguay, its consulate in Buenos Aires was stoned by an angry mob.

Four years later, Uruguay declined to defend their title in Italy. The tournament had adapted a straight knock-out format, and there were 12 finalists from Europe, one from Africa, one from North America, and two from South America. In the semi-finals, Italy beat Austria by a solitary goal and Czechoslovakia put three past Germany. The Final in Rome was a nervous affair, with the teams locked at 1–1 after 90 minutes. A single Italian strike settled it in extra-time.

In 1938, Italy retained the trophy in France. With the threat of another war on the horizon, it was a gloomy, ill-tempered competition featuring 12 European countries, plus Brazil, Cuba and the Dutch East Indies. Italy beat the hosts 3–1 in the second round to reach the last four, where they eliminated Brazil. In the other semi-final, Hungary trounced Sweden 5–1. Italy defeated Hungary 4–2 in the final and the trophy remained in their possession for another 12 years, hidden – during the war – under the bed of a senior Italian federation official, to avoid it being melted down.

Missing the party

England rejoined FIFA after the war, and qualified for six consecutive finals. After 1970, however, they began to stutter. A 2–0 defeat in Poland, in June 1973, followed by an infamous 1–1 draw in the return match at Wembley, four months later, put paid to England's qualification hopes. In May 1974, on the eve of the finals, Alf Ramsey was sacked.

From the start, the 1974 tournament was dogged by controversy, with players threatening to strike over pay amid an atmosphere of political tension and power struggles. Holland, inspired by Johan Cruyff, were a constant beacon of light during a dull competition, putting a disappointing Brazil side to the sword in the quarter-finals. But goals in the final from Gerd Müller and Paul Breitner won the day for West Germany, whose resilience and pragmatism overcame the flair and fluency of Holland's "Total Football".

In 1978, England failed to qualify again. This time coach Don Revie defected to the United Arab Emirates, leaving the national side in disarray and on the verge of elimination. Revie's morose expression had reflected the mood of the times. Isolated at Lancaster Gate, he tried and failed to recreate the team

spirit of Leeds United, with whom he had been so successful, consistently fell out with star players and never fielded a settled side.

A 2–0 defeat by Italy in November 1976 effectively ended England's interest in the World Cup. They flew to Rome unbeaten in the qualifiers, but in the Stadio Olimpico, where they hadn't won since 1961, they were "absolutely murdered" (defender Emlyn Hughes' words). With minutes left and Italy 1–0 up, Roberto Bettega finally put the English out of their misery with a spectacular diving header. Though England, under caretaker boss Ron Greenwood, returned the compliment at Wembley, with goals from Trevor Brooking and Kevin Keegan, the damage had been done.

Pride was restored with qualification in 1982, 1986 and 1990. Then came 1994, and a tortuous campaign under Graham Taylor. In his 38 games between 1990 and 1993, he used 59 players, and at times his tactics and selections were baffling. Devastating defeats in Norway (accompanied by the tabloid newspaper headline "Norse Manure!") and Holland ended Taylor's reign and relegated England to a spectating role during the finals in the USA.

Worse still, it was the tournament to be seen at. Amid a month-long carnival atmosphere, and in front of vast crowds, Brazil cruised through the finals to win the Cup for the first time in 24 years. The final itself was disappointing, as 120 minutes failed to produce a goal. In the penalty shoot-out Brazil beat an injury-plagued Italian team when Roberto Baggio – the World and European player of the year – shot over the crossbar. Back home, the English players, press and public could only look on enviously.

A dejected Paul Gascoigne leaves the field after England's demoralizing defeat in Norway in 1993.

Chapter 6
Stars of the Past

England has produced arguably more legendary footballers than any other country in the world. It was the cradle of the game in the early 1900s, but its first superstars had scant opportunity to test themselves against foreign opposition, limited as it was.

Superstar brothers Jack and Bobby Charlton in 1965.

At the turn of the century, the most famous England international was Steve Bloomer, an inside-right with Derby County who scored 28 goals in 23 games – a record which was finally beaten by Nat Lofthouse in 1956. Alongside him were such celebrated names as Vivian Woodward, a prolific goalscorer for Tottenham Hotspur and Chelsea, right-back and captain Bob Crompton and Liverpool goalkeeper Sam Hardy, the first regular between England's posts.

England had won the Olympic Games football competitions of 1908 and 1912 to stake a claim to be the best of that era. However, the enormous loss of life which followed in World War One changed the world football hierarchy forever.

In the first 33 matches after the Great War, no less than 145 footballers played for England, and there was an average of five changes in the team per game – hardly a model of consistency. Only in the 1930s did England begin to field something approaching a set-

tled side, and it is intriguing to wonder how they would have fared in the first three World Cups.

Would Dixie Dean, for example, have plundered goals against mighty Uruguay or Argentina in 1930? As well as setting goalscoring records at Everton, for whom he netted 60 goals in one season, the awesome centre-forward won 16 caps between 1927 and 1932 and scored 18 goals – 12 in his first five internationals. A few in Montevideo might have made England the first-ever winners of the World Cup.

What might have been

Would Arsenal wing-half Cliff Bastin have performed as well in the 1934 finals as he did against Italy, the soon-to-be-crowned world champions, in a 1–1 draw in Rome in 1933? He scored that day, prompting the Italian crowd to chant, "Basta, Bastin!" ("Enough, Bastin!"). And would the imperious Raich Carter, Sunderland's silver-haired skipper, have torn apart the world's finest defences in France in 1938? Thanks to English football's insular attitude at the time, we will never know.

The war years, too, affected many England players in their prime. Manchester City's Frank Swift kept goal for his country between 1946 and 1949, winning 19 caps, but the charismatic keeper had no opportunity to guard his net against emerging nations like Brazil and Hungary.

But perhaps the unluckiest player of all was Tommy Lawton. In the 1940s, he assumed the mantle of England's top striker, scoring 22 goals in only 23 internationals. Against the Dutch national side in 1946 he became the first Englishman to score four goals in one international, and a year later he scored the fastest goal in his country's history – after 17 seconds in a 10–0 triumph over Portugal in Lisbon. A deadly marksman with Burnley, Everton, Chelsea, Notts County, Brentford and Arsenal, his predatory instinct and powerful heading would surely have taken the World Cup by storm had war not postponed the tournament for 12 years.

Lawton won his last cap in September 1948 against Denmark in Copenhagen when he was only 29 years old. A year later, Walter Winterbottom was preparing to select the first England squad to compete in a qualifying competition for the 1950 World Cup finals.

The man who missed the boat: Tommy Lawton was Engand's top forward for a decade – but he never played in the World Cup.

Bobby **Charlton**

A brilliant body swerve, a ferocious shot – it could only be the legendary Bobby Charlton.

"Now it's Charlton, Bobby Charlton... Hunt on the right... Maybe a shot from Charlton, it's worth trying... And a goal! Thirty-seven minutes. And what a shot from Charlton!"

The commentary was from Kenneth Wolstenholme. The goal was from England's greatest international footballer. Mexico were the opponents, in a group game of the 1966 World Cup. Bobby Charlton had one thought when he received the ball on the edge of the centre-circle in his own half: to run for goal and shoot. He did exactly that, unleashing an unstoppable drive from 30 yards that left the Mexican goalkeeper clutching thin air. England went on to beat France in their last group game and finished top of the group.

Jimmy Greaves described him as "Nureyev on grass." He could shoot with either foot, spray 40-yard passes all over the pitch and run until he dropped. He possessed a wicked body-swerve, often running with the ball from deep as he did against Portugal, bamboozling defenders and letting fly with a thunderbolt.

In all, he scored 49 goals for England – a record which still stands – and until 1973 he was the country's most-capped player. He played in three World Cup final tournaments, making 14 appearances between 1962 and 1970 – only Peter Shilton has played in more. His four hat-tricks equalled the record set by Vivian Woodward at the beginning of the century, and he was the second player (after Steve Bloomer) to set the record for goals as well as appearances.

His record at club level was pretty impressive, too. Born into the famous Milburn clan in the North East, he was always going to be a top-class footballer. He signed for Manchester United as a 15-year-old inside-forward in 1954, scoring twice on his debut two years later (against Charlton Athletic, ironically) and winning the first of three League championships in 1957.

The next year is etched in every football fan's memory: the Munich air disaster claimed the lives of eight Manchester United footballers, but Charlton survived and overcame the tragedy. Within weeks, he was back in action, growing up fast in a decimated United team and scoring against Scotland on his international debut.

Charlton was named in the England squad for the 1958 World Cup finals in Sweden, but he didn't play in the tournament. The subsequent three World Cups were a very different story. In 1962, he was used as a striker, scoring in the 3–1 defeat of Argentina in the first round.

Four years later, he occupied a deeper-lying position and dictated England's play. He was rewarded not just with a World Cup winner's medal, but was voted both England and European Footballer of the Year for 1966. By the time he skippered United to European Cup glory in 1968, he was famous all over the world.

His substitution during the World Cup quarter-final with West Germany in 1970 drew the curtain on an unforgettable 12-year international career.

Bobby CHARLTON

Position: Forward/attacking midfielder
Date of birth: October 11, 1937
Clubs: Manchester United, Preston North End
International debut: vs. Scotland, April 19, 1958 (away, won 4–0)
Last cap: vs. West Germany June 14, 1970 (Leon, lost 2–3)
Appearances: 106
Goals: 49

Jimmy **Greaves**

Natural-born goalscorer: Jimmy Greaves was the most prolific marksman of his generation.

Liverpool striker Robbie Fowler has been likened to Jimmy Greaves more than once. There can be no greater compliment.

It's the best part of 30 years since Greaves hung up his boots, and today's generation of fans know him as "Greavesie", partner of the Saint (Ian St John) and TV pundit. But to those who remember, he was the finest finisher that England has ever produced. He found the net 44 times in 57 internationals – only Bobby Charlton and Gary Lineker have scored more – and he is the only man to score six hat-tricks for England (including one in the 9–3 victory over Scotland at Wembley in 1961).

It was the way he scored goals that caught the eye. He hardly ever blasted his shots – he placed them.

Jimmy GREAVES

Position: Forward
Date of birth: February 20, 1940
Clubs: Chelsea, Milan, Tottenham Hotspur, West Ham United
International debut: vs. Peru, May 17, 1959 (away, lost 1–4)
Last cap: vs. Austria, May 27, 1967 (away, won 1–0)
Appearances: 57
Goals: 44

More often than not, he would receive the ball in the middle of the opponents' half, surge past three or four defenders, dribble around the goalkeeper and slot the ball into the net. Clinical, cool and accurate. A natural, you might say. He scored on his debuts for England and his four clubs, and topped the old First Division scoring charts six times.

Born in London's East End, he scored 124 goals in 157 games for Chelsea before joining Milan in 1961. After four unhappy months in Italy, he was brought back to England for a king's ransom. Tottenham manager Bill Nicholson paid a record £99,999 for his services, and Greaves resumed his role as the deadliest marksman in the game, scoring two goals in the 1963 European Cup-winners Cup final against Atlético Madrid.

He featured in two World Cup tournaments. In Chile, he was a raw 22-year-old with an eye for goal, but England's mediocre form gave him little chance to express himself. In 1966, he was injured against France in England's third match of the tournament and replaced by Geoff Hurst for the subsequent quarter-final against Argentina. Greaves did not return to the side, even when fully fit.

Legend has it, Alf Ramsey felt that Greaves simply didn't work hard enough. But the striker, who was so upset that he boycotted the post-final party, was more candid in his book, *Don't Shoot the Manager*.

"The Saturday of the final came and still I did not know for sure whether I was in or out," he wrote. "But I sensed that Alf was being a little distant, and guessed he had made up his mind not to play me. Sure enough he came to me at around midday and said simply, 'I've decided on an unchanged team. I know you'll understand.' He put his faith at the feet of Hurst, and Geoff came up with an historic hat-trick. Ramsey three, Greaves nil. End of argument."

He won his last cap in 1967 against Austria and made headlines in the 1970s for his battle against the booze. But he will always be remembered as England's most gifted forward – and a joy to behold in full flight.

Bobby Moore

The former West Ham and England midfielder Trevor Brooking has an abiding memory of his team-mate of the early 1970s, Bobby Moore.

"In the dressing-room he followed a meticulous pre-match preparation routine and he was almost obsessively tidy. He folded his clothes neatly and that was how he played – in a cool, calm, neat and tidy manner."

It is fitting, then, that there was some symmetry to the three greatest moments of Moore's career: in 1964, he climbed the famous steps at Wembley to lift the FA Cup after West Ham had beaten Preston North End; in 1965, he climbed them again to receive the European Cup-winners Cup after the London club's victory over Munich 1860; and in 1966, of course, he completed a unique hat-trick by accepting the World Cup from H.M. The Queen in front of 96,924 ecstatic fans. He is best remembered, though, for another image from that same day: the smiling, blond-haired skipper in his red shirt, perched upon his team-mates' shoulders, holding the golden trophy aloft.

A former Footballer of the Year, he was a central defender who exuded authority and composure. He hardly ever made mistakes, and when he did he usually recovered the situation. He wasn't the fastest defender in the world, but he could read the game quicker than most and he never panicked.

Capped 108 times (second only to Peter Shilton in England records), he was a member of three consecutive World Cup teams and was the Player of the Tournament in 1966.

He signed for West Ham in 1958, making his debut at the age of 17. He won 18 caps at England Youth level and made eight appearances for the Under-23 side. His first senior international was against Peru in 1962, and within two years he had taken over the captaincy from Jimmy Armfield. He skippered England 90 times – a world record he still shares with Billy Wright.

Bobby MOORE	
Position:	Centre-half
Date of birth:	May 12, 1941
Clubs:	West Ham United, Fulham
International debut:	vs. Peru, May 20, 1962 (away, won 4–0)
Last cap:	vs. Italy, November 14, 1973, (home, lost 0–1)
Appearances:	108
Goals:	2

In 1966, his understanding with club team-mates Martin Peters and Geoff Hurst was crucial to England's success. At the end of 120 strength-sapping minutes in the final against West Germany, he had the awareness and vision to find Hurst – and set up a goal from the edge of his own penalty area.

Moore won exactly 100 caps under Alf Ramsey, making his final appearance in 1973, the game after England had failed to qualify for the 1974 World Cup finals. He had missed the Poland match, being replaced by Norman Hunter.

Moore was always a gentleman, but he could be ruthless on the pitch when the occasion demanded, as Geoff Hurst recalled: "Someone would come and kick a lump out of him, and he'd play as though he hadn't even noticed. But 10 minutes later – woof! He had a great 'golden boy' image, Mooro. But he was hard."

Robert Frederick Chelsea Moore was many things – not least the supreme defender of his age. Stricken with cancer, he died in 1993.

Elegant and unflappable, Bobby Moore amassed 108 caps for his country over 11 memorable years.

Gordon **Banks**

Guadalajara, Mexico, June 7, 1970. Ten minutes into the eagerly-awaited first-round match between Brazil and England, a 66,000 crowd is about to witness the greatest goalkeeping save of all time.

Brazil are piling on the pressure, and a cross is dispatched toward a familiar, formidable target. "Watch Pele now," roars TV commentator Hugh Johns, as the Brazilian No. 10 soars to meet the ball. He powers his header downward, toward the corner of the England goal. Gordon Banks is beaten, surely – the ball is practically in the net. But no. Somehow, the goalkeeper twists to his right and scoops the ball over the angle of post and crossbar.

There is disbelief on the pitch and in the stands. England captain Bobby Moore, who had stood transfixed by the moment, regains his senses, claps his hands and pats Banks on the head. The save will prove to be in vain as Brazil go on to win the match and the Cup itself.

The Brazilians, like the rest of the world, had nothing but admiration for the Sheffield-born goalkeeper. A few years later, Pele was moved to write, "At that moment I hated Gordon Banks more than any man in soccer. But when I cooled down, I had to applaud him with my heart. It was the greatest save I had ever seen."

Agile and athletic, Gordon Banks was the first in a long line of world-class England goalkeepers.

> **Gordon BANKS**
>
> **Position:** Goalkeeper
> **Date of birth:** December 30, 1937
> **Clubs:** Chesterfield, Leicester City, Stoke City
> **International debut:** vs. Scotland, April 6, 1963 (home, lost 1–2)
> **Last cap:** vs. Scotland, May 27, 1972 (away, won 1–0)
> **Appearances:** 73
> **Clean sheets:** 35

Banks made many great saves during an illustrious career, but none was quite as breathtaking as the one which broke Pele's heart. He may have made more in the 1970 quarter-final against West Germany, but a stomach bug robbed him of a second consecutive appearance in the last eight of the World Cup, and Peter Bonetti deputized in a match that England threw away.

As a teenager with Chesterfield in 1958, Banks could not have foreseen the adulation that awaited him. A modest, quiet and dignified professional throughout his long career, he was snapped up by Leicester City in the early 1960s and gave the club seven years of sterling service, winning the League Cup in 1964 before joining Stoke City for £52,000 – a remarkable fee for a goalkeeper – in 1967. Wherever he played, his shot-stopping was sensational and he always seemed in control.

He won his first cap in 1963 against Scotland and made his last appearance in 1972 against the same opposition. Tragically, a car crash later that year robbed him of his sight in one eye and brought his career to a painfully premature end.

Banks was ever-present during the 1966 World Cup, conceding only three goals in the finals and keeping four clean sheets in a row up to the semi-final match against Portugal, when he was finally beaten by a late Eusebio penalty. In all, he won 73 caps, kept 35 clean sheets and played in 23 consecutive internationals without defeat. A World Cup winner's medal, a 1972 Footballer of the Year award and an OBE sit proudly on his mantelpiece.

Martin **Peters**

Martin Peters is always remembered as the "third" West Ham player to feature in the 1966 World Cup Final. It is, of course, an unfair description. Geoff Hurst got the hat-trick, Bobby Moore got the trophy, but Peters was just as instrumental in England's glory as either of his Upton Park team-mates. He scored the second goal for England after 78 minutes. He was just 22 years old.

In November that year, Charles Buchan's *Football Monthly* magazine recalled his humble beginnings as a footballer. "Cup final contrast for Martin Peters, the West Ham United forward," it reported. "Peters was one of the big successes in England's triumphant World Cup team, and he experienced the tremendous thrill of scoring one of England's four goals against West Germany at Wembley in the final. Compare that with his cup final experience as a member of the Dagenham Boys team. Martin, who attended Fanshawe School in Dagenham, played in two boys' cup finals, and gave an own-goal away each time!"

Evidently, those early gaffes merely spurred Peters on to greater things. They may even have speeded up his development. Alf Ramsey famously hailed Peters as 10 years ahead of his time. It was a tag that remained with him throughout his playing days, which took in spells with the Hammers, Tottenham Hotspur and Norwich City, as well as 67 caps for his country. But it was highly appropriate.

Deceptively slight, he possessed all the assets of the modern footballer: athleticism, pace, power, intuition and versatility. And like David Platt after him, he acquired the priceless knack of arriving late in the penalty area to score goals – 20 for England during an eight-year international career and 80 in 300 games for West Ham.

Peters could score and create with ease, but if anything he was under-rated by his contemporaries, perhaps because he was so diligent and shunned the limelight. Ramsey, however, knew a class act when he saw one.

Peters made his debut for England against Yugoslavia just two months before the 1966 finals, and his industry, adaptability and astute reading of the game did not go unnoticed by the coaching staff. Although predominantly right-footed, he played on the left flank during the final tournament, tormenting opponents by haring down the wing or cutting inside to create chances for Hurst and Bobby Charlton. He was made captain for Ramsey's last game in charge, in April 1974 against Portugal, and made his final appearance for England against Scotland later that year.

At club-level, his many talents were guarded jealously by West Ham, for whom he played in every position, filling in as a defender, midfielder, striker and even goalkeeper. In 1970, he became British football's first £200,000 player when he moved from the Hammers to Tottenham, with Jimmy Greaves going the other way. At White Hart Lane, he won the UEFA Cup in 1972 before a troublesome Achilles injury limited his appearances and he ended his career at Carrow Road.

Martin PETERS

Position: Attacking midfielder
Date of birth: November 8, 1943
Clubs: West Ham United, Tottenham Hotspur, Norwich City
International debut: vs. Yugoslavia, May 4, 1966 (home, won 2–0)
Last cap: vs. Scotland, May 18, 1974 (away, lost 0–2)
Appearances: 67
Goals: 20

Martin Peters scores England's second goal in the 1966 final.

Peter Shilton: a record-breaking goalkeeper.

Peter **Shilton**

Peter Shilton was a perfectionist between the posts. Loud and authoritative from an early age, he recognized that only sporting excellence would propel him to the top of his profession, and to this end he put himself through punishing training schedules throughout his long and fulfilling career.

His dedication paid off handsomely, and his achievements are phenomenal. He holds the world record for the most appearances by an international footballer for England – 125 – over half of which were clean sheets, between 1970 and 1990. Had coach Ron Greenwood not rotated him with Liverpool's Ray Clemence in goal, it would have been many more. Only Stanley Matthews enjoyed a longer career with his country.

Shilton played in three consecutive World Cup finals (1982, 1986 and 1990), making a British record 17 appearances, while his 10 clean sheets beat the previous benchmark set by West Germany's Sepp Maier

Peter SHILTON

Position: Goalkeeper
Date of birth: September 18, 1949
Clubs: Leicester City, Stoke City, Nottingham Forest, Southampton, Derby County, Plymouth Argyle, Bolton Wanderers, Leyton Orient
International debut: vs. East Germany, November 25, 1970 (home, won 3–1)
Last cap: vs. Italy, July 7, 1990 (Bari, lost 1–2)
Appearances: 125
Clean sheets: 66

1970–78. During the 1982 finals in Spain, he came within 90 minutes of equalling Gordon Banks' national record of seven consecutive matches without conceding a goal.

And when he wasn't breaking records for England, he clocked up 1,005 league appearances with Leicester City, Stoke City, Nottingham Forest, Southampton, Derby County, Plymouth Argyle (where he was player manager), Bolton Wanderers and Leyton Orient. In 1996–97 he became the first player ever to appear in 1,000 Football League matches.

He began his goalkeeping odyssey as an understudy to Banks at Filbert Street in the early 1960s. Legend has it, the great man left for Stoke City in 1967 after his precocious deputy vowed to walk out if he wasn't picked ahead of the England goalkeeper! It was a measure of Shilton's burning ambition to succeed, but he was the first to acknowledge that he learned his trade under Banks. Later in his career, he was to follow in his mentor's footsteps as a goalkeeper with Stoke.

He made his debut for England against East Germany in November 1970. By the time he had established himself as the national team's No. 1, Shilton was a model of concentration and consistency. He would often stay behind after club training sessions for extra practice. In his penalty area, he was a commanding presence, and he would warm up strenuously in the dressing-room before kick-off to guard against complacency at the start of every match.

At club level, he enjoyed his most successful period in the late 1970s, when he won the League Championship, European Cup (twice) and Footballer of the Year award with Nottingham Forest.

He made his final appearance for England in the 1990 World Cup third-place play-off against Italy, and was appointed skipper for the match by Bobby Robson as a mark of recognition for his outstanding service to England and English football in general. His place in football's hall of fame is guaranteed, and his huge international appearance haul is unlikely to be surpassed.

Kevin **Keegan**

Kevin Keegan was a man of many talents. Not only did he play 63 times for his country, scoring 21 goals, he is also the only England international to croon his way into the Top Ten as a solo singer (Hoddle and Waddle were a duo) with a 1978 single called "Head Over Heels". It was just one more success story in the career of the premier sporting celebrity of the 1970s.

Keegan was also the ultimate professional. He was blessed with single-minded determination, rather than outright flair, and he worked hard to reach the top of the tree with Liverpool and England. Rejected as a youngster by Coventry City, he joined his local club Scunthorpe United and vowed to improve himself as a footballer.

Stories abound of him running up and down the Scunthorpe terraces carrying weights after normal training had ended. By his own admission, when he joined Liverpool in 1971 for a modest £35,000 (Reds boss Bill Shankly called it "robbery without violence"), he was already the fittest player at his new club.

With Liverpool, he won three League titles, the FA Cup, the UEFA Cup and the European Cup in the space of only six years. He had always harboured an ambition to play abroad, and when Hamburg expressed an interest in 1977, it was an offer he could not refuse. While in Germany, Keegan won consecutive European Footballer of the Year awards, 1978–79, but he returned to England in the 1980s to play for Southampton and Newcastle United, for whom he would return once more as a manager and messiah.

Though he was an automatic choice and regular goalscorer for England in his prime, Keegan's international career never quite took off. Having made his debut in November 1972 against Wales, he tried and failed to help England qualify for the 1974 and 1978 World Cup finals. In either tournament, he would surely have been a star, but on both occasions England were hopelessly inept in their qualifying group.

His first – and last – chance for World Cup

Kev strikes again! He scored 21 goals in 63 games during a 10-year international career.

glory came in 1982, under Ron Greenwood, but a persistent back problem ruled him out of England's first four games. In the week before the all-important tie against Spain in the second round – a match that England had to win – he was so desperate to play that he persuaded Greenwood to let him slip out of the team hotel one night, drive from Bilbao to Madrid and fly in secret back to Hamburg to see a specialist.

He was away for two days, returning to take part in the last 25 minutes of the game. Within seconds, he had a golden opportunity to put England ahead, but he headed wide with the goal at his mercy. Little did he know that it was his last appearance for England: when Bobby Robson succeeded Greenwood in 1982, he omitted the stocky striker from his first squad. Keegan vowed never to play for England again.

Kevin KEEGAN

Position: Forward

Date of birth: February 14, 1951

Clubs: Scunthorpe United, Liverpool, Hamburg, Southampton, Newcastle United

International debut: vs. Wales, November 15, 1972 (away, won 1–0)

Last cap: vs. Spain, July 5, 1982 (Madrid, drew 0–0)

Appearances: 63

Goals: 21

Trevor **Brooking**

Nicknamed "Hadleigh" by Kevin Keegan because of his chiselled features and impeccable manners, similar to a television character of the time, Trevor Brooking was an elegant midfielder who strutted his stuff on the world stage for 12 years.

He was a graduate of West Ham's famous "Academy of Football", following in the tradition of Bobby Moore, Geoff Hurst and Martin Peters, and he was capped 47 times between 1974 and 1982, scoring five goals. Like Keegan, he was injured during his one and only World Cup finals tournament and managed

survivors (along with Bonds and Lampard) from the team which had beaten Fulham in the 1975 final, Brooking scored the only goal of the game against the Gunners, stooping to head home a low, mis-directed shot from David Cross after 10 minutes.

The odds against him scoring the first goal of that FA Cup final had been 16–1, but no one imagined that he might get it with his head. Brooking also received a League Cup runners-up medal in 1981 after defeat by Liverpool in a replay at Villa Park.

Although he made his England debut in the last few months of Don Revie's reign, it was under Ron Greenwood, his old boss at West Ham, that he thrived as an international, combining on more than one

Trevor BROOKING

Position: Attacking midfielder
Date of birth: October 2, 1948
Clubs: West Ham United
International debut: vs. Portugal, April 3, 1974 (away, drew 0–0)
Last cap: vs. Spain, July 5, 1982 (Madrid, drew 0–0)
Appearances: 47
Goals: 5

A classy midfielder and a model of sportsmanship, Brooking was never sent off for club or country.

just 20 minutes in the second-round game against Spain which ended his country's interest in the competition.

He was a one-club man, staying at Upton Park throughout his 17-year career and starring in an exciting side which also included Alan Devonshire, Frank Lampard Senior and Billy Bonds. Skilful and creative, he provided the Hammers with an extra dimension in midfield, but his love for the club and enthusiasm for the game never boiled over into aggression. He was booked just five times and never sent off.

Having joined the East End club in July 1965, he proceeded to play 637 first-team games before retiring in 1984. He appeared in two FA Cup finals, and West Ham fans have fond memories of his contribution in the final against Arsenal in 1980. One of only three

occasion with Keegan to find the back of the net.

He is perhaps best remembered for the goal that he scored against Hungary in Budapest during a 3–1 qualifying group victory which virtually booked England's place in the 1982 World Cup finals. After a scintillating England move, he let fly from the edge of the box and his fierce left-foot shot beat the goalkeeper and ended up wedged behind the stanchion holding up the net – sweet revenge for the two embarrassing defeats that the Magyars dished out to England in the 1950s.

Upon his retirement as a player, he stayed in the public eye, as a television and radio pundit. In between the odd spot of charity work in East London, where he is still regarded as a local hero, he provides weekly analysis on BBC's "Match of the Day".

Bryan **Robson**

It is something of a wonder that Bryan Robson is still standing. During a long and distinguished playing career, he suffered around 20 breaks or dislocations, including a broken leg three times from 1976.

Injuries routinely prevented the man they nick-named "Captain Marvel" from landing even more honours. But he never shirked a tackle, whether for Manchester United or England – his will to win and unquenchable spirit just would not allow it.

Despite his regular visits to the treatment room, Robson made 90 international appearances and skippered his country 65 times – only Billy Wright and Bobby Moore have captained England more often. He ranks fifth in appearances and seventh – with 26 – in goals in England's all-time records, and scored the second fastest goal ever in the World Cup finals. After 27 seconds of the match against France in 1982, he smashed home England's opener after a pre-rehearsed move from a throw-in – one of three occasions on which Robson scored in the opening minute.

Robson was always destined for great things. He earned his spurs as a midfielder under Ron Atkinson at West Bromwich Albion in the late 1970s. When Atkinson was appointed manager of Manchester United in 1981, there was only one signing he wanted to make. In August that year, Robson moved to Old Trafford for a British record £1.5 million.

He had already made his international debut – against the Republic of Ireland in a European Championship qualifier at Wembley – and at United he cemented his reputation as an all-action midfielder, winning the ball, setting up attacks and scoring goals. He won the FA Cup three times and the League Championship twice, as United gradually evolved from a team of expensive misfits into the most fearsome outfit in England. Every one of United's current crop of superstars will say they learned from Robson.

Although injury wreaked havoc with his career at club and international level, he was always an automatic choice for captain when fit and was never once named as an England substitute. The national team was all the poorer for his absence in 1986 and 1990, but his enthusiasm rubbed off on everyone in the camp – so much so that Terry Venables invited Robson to join his coaching staff between 1994 and 1996 while he was also managing Middlesbrough.

Robson played to win and injuries were merely an

Bryan Robson overcame countless injuries to captain his country on 65 occasions.

occupational hazard. "When I broke my leg for the third time, I did think, 'Crikey, here we go again'," he later reflected. "I got my dislocated shoulder when I was running to head a ball and I landed on an icy part of the pitch at Old Trafford and went over the hoardings.

"When the ball's there and the adrenalin's going in a game, I always just dived into tackles. But my injuries were highlighted because two of them were in World Cups, and you can't really get any more high-profile than that."

Bryan ROBSON

Position: Midfielder
Date of birth: January 1, 1957
Clubs: West Bromwich Albion, Manchester United, Middlesbrough
International debut: vs. Republic of Ireland, February 6, 1980 (home, won 2–0)
Last cap: vs. Republic of Ireland, March 27, 1991 (home, drew 1–1)
Appearances: 90
Goals: 26

John **Barnes**

Scoring a wonder goal for England against Brazil in the Maracana Stadium might have been a thrilling achievement at the time, but it was probably the worst thing that could have happened to John Barnes. For the rest of his international career, he had to live up to that magic moment, and the expectations of the England crowd often turned to frustration and, ultimately, criticism.

Having made his debut in 1983 against Northern Ireland in a friendly, Barnes took the footballing world by storm during England's 1984 tour of South America by weaving through the Brazilian defence to score the opening goal in an historic 2–0 victory.

From then on, he was always in the spotlight. "While I was in Rio a photographer asked me to juggle the ball on Copacabana beach," he recalled. "I felt so embarrassed – we were surrounded by kids who could juggle the ball so much better than me!"

It was a typically laid-back response from a player who remained philosophical about the direction of his career. Born in Jamaica, the son of a military attaché, he was a firm believer in fate.

"I believe that everything in life is mapped out for you," he later said. "Why else would I have ruptured my Achilles tendon at a time when I was interested in moving abroad? If I was meant to have moved to Italy or France or Spain, I would have gone."

Barnes had always maintained that he wanted to pit his wits against Europe's finest, and it was with some reluctance that he joined Liverpool from Watford for £900,000 as a 23-year-old winger in 1987. He had spent six seasons under Graham Taylor at Vicarage Road, reaching double figures in the scoring charts every year, winning promotion to the old First Division and playing in the 1984 FA Cup Final against Everton.

At Anfield, the goals kept coming and he won a League Championship medal and the Footballer of the Year award in a dazzling first season. But he still fancied his chances abroad… until that injury – sustained while playing for England – dashed any lingering hopes of a new career on the Continent.

A total of 10 goals in 79 internationals is a poor return for a footballer of his stature, but he was unable to express himself as freely for England as he could with Liverpool, for whom he was allowed to drift in from the wing. Arguably his best England performance was also his shortest: against Argentina in the 1986 World Cup finals, he came on as a late substitute and ran the South Americans ragged, crossing for Gary Lineker to score.

Seven years later, he reached his lowest ebb as an England player during the World Cup qualifier with San Marino at Wembley, when his every touch was cruelly booed by a home crowd which had run out of patience. He remains one of the most gifted individuals to wear the white shirt, if not the most successful.

John BARNES

Position: Forward/ midfielder
Date of birth: November 7, 1963
Clubs: Watford, Liverpool, Newcastle United
International debut: vs. Northern Ireland, May 28, 1983 (away, drew 0–0)
Last cap: vs. Colombia, September 6, 1995 (home, drew 0–0)
Appearances: 79
Goals: 11

Flawed genius? Barnes never quite reproduced his club form at international level.

Gary Lineker

Goalscoring is all about timing, composure, intuition and accuracy. Gary Winston Lineker had them all. He was England's finest poacher since Jimmy Greaves, and like all great marksmen, he made it look easy.

He was at Leicester City when he made his international debut, coming on as a substitute for Tony Woodcock in a friendly against Scotland at Hampden Park. Although Leicester was his home-town club, his prolific goalscoring was always going to attract attention, and in 1985 he moved to League Champions Everton for £800,000.

Lineker was an instant hit at Goodison Park, scoring 30 goals as Everton came desperately close to pulling off the elusive League and Cup 'Double'. He was in irresistible form, and it was no surprise when Bobby Robson chose him to spearhead England's attack in the 1986 World Cup finals.

Goals were his business: Gary Lineker's poaching instinct carved out many a memorable victory.

Just 10 days before the first game in Mexico, he sprained his wrist in a friendly against Canada and had to wear a protective plaster. The same arm would be raised aloft in celebration six times during England's World Cup campaign. He combined with Everton team-mates Peter Reid and Gary Stevens to pounce on Poland with a first-half hat-trick which booked his team's place in the second round, where he scored twice against Paraguay. In the quarter-finals, it was his late goal which gave England hope against Argentina. His goals earned him FIFA's Golden Boot, and back home he picked up the Player of the Year award.

Again, he was a wanted man, and Catalan giants Barcelona swooped with a £2.75 million bid to prise him away from Everton after just one season on Merseyside. Tottenham brought him home in a £1.1 million deal in 1989, and he won the FA Cup with Spurs two years later, before ending his career in the Japanese league with Nagoya Grampus Eight.

Wherever he played, Lineker always came up with the goods for his country. His 48 goals in 80 games (including 23 in his first 25 internationals) is second only to Bobby Charlton. He scored the only goal in a game on 16 occasions and was the first England striker to score more than one hat-trick since Geoff Hurst. He scored 10 goals in two World Cups: six in 1986 – he is the only British player to be a World Cup finals top scorer – and four in 1990.

Lineker was England's captain from manager Graham Taylor's first game in charge, but his international career ended on a sour note when Taylor replaced him during a European Championship finals tie with Sweden in 1992. It was a match which England had to win and he was just one goal away from equalling Charlton's goalscoring record. He would never play for England again.

Nevertheless, he is fondly remembered for the World Cup hat-trick against the Poles in 1986 and the semi-final equalizer against West Germany in 1990. He is now a prominent television and radio personality.

> **Gary LINEKER**
>
> **Position:** Forward
> **Date of birth:** November 30, 1960
> **Clubs:** Leicester City, Everton, Barcelona, Tottenham Hotspur, Nagoya Grampus Eight
> **International debut:** vs. Scotland, May 26, 1984 (away, drew 1–1)
> **Last cap:** vs. Sweden, June 17, 1992 (Stockholm, lost 1–2)
> **Appearances:** 80
> **Goals:** 48

David **Platt**

So there's no such thing as an overnight success? Try telling that to David Platt.

The morning after an eventful June evening in 1990, his life had changed completely. From being a late – and relatively unknown – choice for the England squad, he had become world-famous and a wanted man. That's what scoring a last-second, match-winning goal in the World Cup finals can do for you.

Time was almost up in England's second-round match against Belgium in Bologna when Paul Gascoigne lofted a free-kick into the penalty area and Platt connected sweetly to score with a fantastic overhead volley. For the Oldham-born midfielder, nothing was ever going to be the same again. He would be returning to Italy sooner than he thought, with Bari heading the queue of exotic clubs after his signature.

He had made his debut for England, seven months before the World Cup, against Italy at Wembley. A superb spell with Aston Villa, for whom he scored 19 goals (including one against Internazionale in the UEFA Cup) for the second successive season, caught the eye of the England management and he was called up. After a limited involvement in first-round matches, three goals in the knock-out stages – against the Belgians, Cameroon and Italy (he was England's second-highest scorer in the tournament behind Gary Lineker) – propelled him into the limelight and on to the back pages.

He later admitted that his dizzy rise to stardom did take its toll. "When I got into the England World Cup 1990 side I was only a squad player. Then – bang! I scored a goal against Belgium and for four or five months I'm not handling the situation – the situation is handling me. Everyone wants to speak to me and I'm recognized all over the world. For three or four months, I'll admit it, it got hold of me and I didn't have it under control. Eventually, I got it under control and relished it."

In the process, Platt became the world's most expensive footballer in terms of combined transfer

> ### David PLATT
> **Position:** Midfielder
> **Date of birth:** June 10, 1966
> **Clubs:** Crewe Alexandra, Aston Villa, Bari, Sampdoria, Juventus, Arsenal
> **International debut:** vs. Italy, November 15, 1989 (home, drew 0–0)
> **Last cap:** vs. Germany, June 26, 1996 (Wembley, drew 1–1, lost on pens)
> **Appearances:** 62
> **Goals:** 27

One of the stars of the 1990 World Cup, David Platt went on to win 62 caps, scoring 27 goals.

fees. Already an established star for England, he moved from Bari to Sampdoria to Juventus to Arsenal for a total in excess of £20 million. A tireless runner and prodigious worker, he learned to play a more disciplined, defensive game in Italy.

But his speciality at international level was surging forward from deep positions to score vital goals – 27 in 62 matches, including nine in nine games during one purple patch in 1993. His finishing was precise, and his heading ability was exceptional.

Had England qualified for the 1994 World Cup finals in the USA, he would doubtless have enjoyed more success at the peak of his career. But that failure under Graham Taylor, followed by the new regime of Terry Venables, signalled the beginning of the end of his England career.

"I had seven very good years at international level, including being captain," he remarked. "Nobody can take those away from me."

Chapter 7
World Cup Records

Quarter-finalists six times, semi-finalists twice, winners once. England's World Cup record since 1950 has been one of peaks and troughs. They declined to compete in the first three tournaments, and their progress was hardly inspiring when they finally entered the competition in 1950 – they were eliminated in the first round.

Four years later England reached the quarter-finals, but in 1958 they were knocked out in the early stages once more. In their fourth successive tournament, they redeemed themselves by reaching the last eight again, but there was little to suggest that they could actually win the World Cup. The appointment of Alf Ramsey as coach changed all that, and 1966 remains England's finest hour.

A third quarter-final appearance – in Mexico in 1970 – was followed by 12 bleak years in the international wilderness, when successive England sides failed to qualify for the tournaments in West Germany and Argentina. Elimination in the second round in 1982 did little to restore morale, but progress to the quarter-finals and semi-finals respectively in the next two tournaments seemed to indicate that England were back on course for footballing greatness.

Then came 1994 and a disastrous qualifying campaign which undid all the previous good work. The boat has since been steadied, of course, and France 1998 will be England's 10th appearance in finals. They remain one of only six countries to win the trophy and are currently fifth in the all-time World Cup ranking behind Brazil, Germany, Italy and Argentina.

After mediocre performances in their first four World Cups, England went all the way in 1966. They have yet to repeat the feat.

World Cup Results

1950 BRAZIL

Qualifying Group One
Wales 1, England 4
England 9, Northern Ireland 2
Scotland 0, England 1

Final Tournament First Round
England 2 (Mortensen 37, Mannion 52), Chile 0
USA 1, England 0
Spain 1, England 0

Group Two

	P	W	D	L	F	A	Pts
Spain	3	3	0	0	6	1	6
England	3	1	0	2	2	2	2
Chile	3	1	0	2	5	6	2
USA	3	1	0	2	4	8	2

1954 SWITZERLAND

Qualifying Group Three
Wales 1, England 4   England 3, Northern Ireland 1
Scotland 2, England 4

Final Tournament First Round
England 4 (Broadis 26, 63, Lofthouse 36, 91), Belgium 4
England 2 (Mullen 43, Wilshaw 69), Switzerland 0

Group Four

	P	W	D	L	F	A	Pts
England	2	1	1	0	6	4	3
Italy	2	1	0	1	5	3	2
Switzerland	2	1	0	1	2	3	2
Belgium	2	0	1	1	5	8	1

Quarter-finals
Uruguay 4, England 2 (Lofthouse 16, Finney 67)

1958 SWEDEN

Qualifying Group One
England 5, Denmark 2   England 5, Rep. of Ireland 1
Denmark 1, England 4   Rep. of Ireland 1, England 1

Final Tournament First Round
England 2 (Kevan 66, Finney 85), USSR 2
Brazil 0, England 0
England 2 (Haynes 56, Kevan 78), Austria 2

Group Four

	P	W	D	L	F	A	Pts
Brazil	3	2	1	0	5	0	5
USSR	3	1	1	1	4	4	3
England	3	0	3	0	4	4	3
Austria	3	0	1	2	2	7	1

Play-off for Quarter-finals
USSR 1, England 0

1962 CHILE

Qualifying Group Six
Luxembourg 0, England 9   Portugal 1, England 1
England 4, Luxembourg 1   England 2, Portugal 0

Final Tournament First Round
Hungary 2, England 1 (Flowers 60)
England 3 (Flowers 14, R. Charlton 42, Greaves 57), Argentina 1
England 0, Bulgaria 0

Group Four

	P	W	D	L	F	A	Pts
Hungary	3	2	1	0	8	2	5
England	3	1	1	1	4	3	3
Argentina	3	1	1	1	2	3	3
Bulgaria	3	0	1	2	1	7	1

Quarter-finals
Brazil 3, England 1 (Hitchens 38)

1966 ENGLAND (QUALIFIED AS HOSTS)

Final Tournament First Round
England 0, Uruguay 0
England 2 (R. Charlton 37, Hunt 75), Mexico 0
England 2 (Hunt 38, 75), France 0

Group One

	P	W	D	L	F	A	Pts
England	3	2	1	0	4	0	5
Uruguay	3	1	2	0	2	1	4
Mexico	3	0	2	1	1	3	2
France	3	0	1	2	2	5	1

Quarter-finals
England 1 (Hurst 78), Argentina 0

Semi-finals
England 2 (R. Charlton 30, 79), Portugal 1

Final
England 4 (Hurst 19, 100, 119, Peters 77), West Germany 2

1970 MEXICO (QUALIFIED AS CHAMPIONS)

Final Tournament First Round
England 1 (Hurst 65), Romania 0
Brazil 1, England 0
England 1 (Clarke 50), Czechoslovakia 0

Group Three

	P	W	D	L	F	A	Pts
Brazil	3	3	0	0	8	3	6
England	3	2	0	1	2	1	4
Romania	3	1	0	2	4	5	2
Czech.	3	0	0	3	2	7	0

Quarter-finals
West Germany 3, England 2 (Mullery 31, Peters 49)

1982 SPAIN

Qualifying Group Four

England 4, Norway 0	Romania 2, England 1
England 2, Switzerland 1	England 0, Romania 0
Switzerland 2, England 1	Hungary 1, England 3
Norway 2, England 1	England 1, Hungary 0

Final Tournament First Round

England 3 (Robson 1, 66, Mariner 82), France 1
England 2 (Francis 63, og 66), Czechoslovakia 0
England 1 (Francis 27), Kuwait 0

Group Four

	P	W	D	L	F	A	Pts
England	3	3	0	0	6	1	6
France	3	1	1	1	6	5	3
Czech.	3	0	2	1	2	4	2
Kuwait	3	0	1	2	2	6	1

Second Round

West Germany 0, England 0
England 0, Spain 0

Group B

	P	W	D	L	F	A	Pts
West Germany	2	1	1	0	2	1	3
England	2	0	2	0	0	0	2
Spain	2	0	1	1	1	2	1

1986 MEXICO

Qualifying Group Three

England 5, Finland 0	Turkey 0, England 8
Northern Ireland 0, England 1	Romania 0, England 0
Finland 1, England 1	England 1, Romania 1
England 5, Turkey 0	England 0, Northern Ireland 0

Final Tournament First Round

Portugal 1, England 0
Morocco 0, England 0
England 3 (Lineker 7, 13, 36), Poland 0

Group Six

	P	W	D	L	F	A	Pts
Morocco	3	1	2	0	3	1	4
England	3	1	1	1	3	1	3
Poland	3	1	1	1	1	3	3
Portugal	3	1	0	2	2	4	2

Second Round

England 3 (Lineker 31, 72, Beardsley 55), Paraguay 0

Quarter-finals

Argentina 2, England 1 (Lineker 81)

1990 ITALY

Qualifying Group Two

England 0, Sweden 0	Albania 0, England 2
England 5, Albania 0	England 3, Poland 0
Sweden 0, England 0	Poland 0, England 0

Final Tournament First Round

England 1 (Lineker 8), Rep. of Ireland 1
England 0, Holland 0
England 1 (Wright 58) Egypt 0

Group F

	P	W	D	L	F	A	Pts
England	3	1	2	0	2	1	4
Rep. of Ireland	3	0	3	0	2	2	3
Holland	3	0	3	0	2	2	3
Egypt	3	0	2	1	1	2	2

Second Round

England 1 (Platt 119), Belgium 0

Quarter-finals

England 3 (Platt 25, Lineker 82, 105), Cameroon 2

Semi-finals

West Germany 1, England 1 (Lineker 80)
West Germany won 4–3 on penalties

Third-place Play-off

Italy 2, England 1 (Platt 80)

TOTAL RECORD IN FINAL TOURNAMENTS

Played	Won	Drawn	Lost	Goals for	against
41	18	12	11	55	38

Fifth in all-time World Cup ranking 1930–94

Gary Lineker: the only Englishman to finish a finals tournament as top scorer. His six goals in 1986 earned him the accolade.

Miscellaneous World Cup Records

WORLD CUP RECORDS

Overall Performance

1930	Did not enter	1970	Quarter-finals
1934	Did not enter	1974	Failed to qualify
1938	Did not enter	1978	Failed to qualify
1950	First Round	1982	Second Round
1954	Quarter-finals	1986	Quarter-finals
1958	First Round	1990	Semi-finals
1962	Quarter-finals	1994	Failed to qualify
1966	Winners		

Most Appearances in Final Tournaments

3	Billy Wright	1950, 1954, 1958
3	Tom Finney	1950, 1954, 1958
3	Bobby Charlton	1962, 1966, 1970
3	Bobby Moore	1962, 1966, 1970
3	Terry Butcher	1982, 1986, 1990
3	Bryan Robson	1982, 1986, 1990
3	Peter Shilton	1982, 1986, 1990

WORLD CUP RECORDS

Most Goals in Finals Tournaments

10	Gary Lineker	1986, 1990
5	Geoff Hurst	1966, 1970
4	Bobby Charlton	1962, 1966

Most Goals in One Final Tournament

6	Gary Lineker	1986
4	Geoff Hurst	1966
4	Gary Lineker	1990
3	Nat Lofthouse	1954
3	Roger Hunt	1966
3	Bobby Charlton	1966
3	David Platt	1990

Biggest Win in the Finals

England 3 Poland 0	1986
England 3 Paraguay 0	1986

Paul Gascoigne weaves his way through the West German defence in the 1990 semi-final.

WORLD CUP RECORDS

Most Appearances in Final Tournaments

17	Peter Shilton	1982, 1990
14	Bobby Charlton	1962, 1970
14	Bobby Moore	1962, 1970
14	Terry Butcher	1982, 1990
12	Gary Lineker	1986, 1990
11	Chris Waddle	1986, 1990
10	Billy Wright	1950, 1958
10	Ray Wilson	1962, 1966

Hat-tricks in Final Tournaments

Geoff Hurst vs. West Germany	1966
Gary Lineker vs. Poland	1986

Biggest Win in the Qualifiers

Luxembourg 0, England 9	1962

Biggest Win in the Finals

England 3, Poland 0	1986
England 3, Paraguay 0	1986

Biggest Defeat in the Qualifiers

Poland 2, England 0	1974
Italy 2, England 0	1978
Holland 2, England 0	1993
Norway 2, England 0	1993

Biggest defeat in the Finals

Uruguay 4, England 2	1954
Brazil 3, England 1	1962

WORLD CUP RECORDS

Captains

1950	Billy Wright
1954	Billy Wright
1958	Billy Wright
1962	Johnny Haynes
1966	Bobby Moore
1970	Bobby Moore
1982	Mick Mills
1986	Bryan Robson, Peter Shilton
1990	Bryan Robson, Terry Butcher, Peter Shilton

Coaches

1950	Walter Winterbottom
1954	Walter Winterbottom
1958	Walter Winterbottom
1962	Walter Winterbottom
1966	Alf Ramsey
1970	Alf Ramsey
1982	Ron Greenwood
1986	Bobby Robson
1990	Bobby Robson

General England Records

GENERAL ENGLAND RECORDS

Coaches

1946–62	Walter Winterbottom
1963–74	Alf Ramsey
1974	Joe Mercer
1974–77	Don Revie
1977–82	Ron Greenwood
1982–90	Bobby Robson
1990–93	Graham Taylor
1994–96	Terry Venables
1996–	Glenn Hoddle

Most International Appearances

125	Peter Shilton	1970–90
108	Bobby Moore	1962–73
106	Bobby Charlton	1958–70
105	Billy Wright	1946–59
90	Bryan Robson	1980–91
86	Kenny Sansom	1979–88
84	Ray Wilkins	1976–86
80	Gary Lineker	1984–92
79	John Barnes	1983–95
77	Terry Butcher	1980–90

GENERAL ENGLAND RECORDS

Most International Goals

Bobby Charlton	49	106 games, 1958–70
Gary Lineker	48	80 games, 1984–92
Jimmy Greaves	44	57 games, 1959–67
Tom Finney	30	76 games, 1946–58
Nat Lofthouse	30	33 games, 1950–58
Vivian Woodward	29	23 games, 1903–11
Steve Bloomer	23	25 games, 1895–1907
David Platt	27	62 games, 1989–96
Bryan Robson	26	90 games, 1980–91
Geoff Hurst	24	49 games, 1966–72

With 125 appearances, Peter Shilton is by far the most-capped England international of all time.

Index

Entries in *italics* refer to pictures

A

Adams, Tony 13, *14*, 15, 16, 18, 21, 25, 39, 43, *43*, 46
Albert, Florian 74
Albertini, Demetrio 46, 47
Anderton, Darren 52
Argentina 28, 29, 30, 31, 68, 74, 77, 82, 83, *83*, 88–9, 92, 93, 101, 102, 104
Armfield, Jimmy 74, 94
Arsenal 13, 39, 43, 55, 57, 61, 91, 99, 103
Asprilla, Faustino 31
Astle, Jeff 78
Aston Villa 46, 103
Atkinson, Ron 100
Atletico Madrid 93
Austria 67, 70, 71, 73, 88, 89, 93

B

Baggio, Dino 47
Baggio, Roberto 89
Bahr, Walter 69
Bakhramov, Tofik 76
Ball, Alan 76, 77
Banks, Gordon 38, 76, 78, 79, 95, *95*, 97
Barcelona 102
Bari 103
Barmby, Nick 10, 61
Barnes, John 52, 65, 83, 101, *101*
Barnes, Peter 80
Bastin, Cliff 90
Batty, David 15, 16, *17*, 18, 20, 21, 24, 25, *36*, 47, *47*, 49
Beardsley, Peter 51, 52, 65, 82, *82*, 83, 86, 87
Beckenbauer, Franz 45, 79, 87
Beckham, David 9, 11, 12, *15*,

18, 20, 21, 24, 25, 37, *37*, 41, 49, 50, *50*, 54, 61
Belgium 30, 71, 87, *87*, 88, 103
Bell, Colin 78, 79
Bennarivo, Antonio 46
Bettega, Roberto 89
Birmingham City 39
Blackburn Rovers 38, 42, 47, 55
Blackpool 68
Blanchflower, Danny 60
Blatter, Sepp 29
Bloomer, Steve 90, 92
Bolton Wanderers 97
Bonds, Billy 99
Bonetti, Peter 79, 95
Brazil 22, 28, 29, 30, 32, 33, 34, 38, 40, 41, 60, 65, 68, 69, 72, 73, 74, 75, 77, 78, *78*, 79, *79*, 89, 91, 95, 101, 104
Brehme, Andreas 87
Breitner, Paul 89
Brentford 91
Broadis, Ivan *70*, 71
Brooking, Trevor 59, 80, 81, 89, 94, 99, *99*
Buchwald, Guido 87
Bulgaria 60, 74
Bull, Steve 30
Burnley 91
Butcher, Terry 80, 81, 86, 87
Byrne, Roger 72

C

Calderwood, Colin 61
Cameroon 35, 45, 87, 103
Campbell, Sol 15, 16, 18, 21, 24, 25, 34, 44, *44*
Canada 68, 82, 102
Cannavaro, Fabio *16*
Carlos, Alberto 32, 34
Carter, Raich 91
Castro, Hector 89
Celtic 52

Charlton Athletic 92
Charlton brothers 41
Charlton brothers *90*
Charlton, Bobby 73, 74, 75, 76, 78, 79, *90*, 92, *92*, 93, 96, 102
Charlton, Jack 76, 86, *90*
Chelsea 8, 17, 24, 31, 42, 61, 90, 91, 93
Chesterfield 95
Chiesa, Enrico 25, 44
Chile 69
China 41
Chivadze, Alexander 13
Citko, Marek 11
Clarke, Allan 78
Clemence, Ray 38, 59, 97
Clough, Brian 72, 80
Cohen, George 76
Cole, Andy 57
Colombia 28, *28*, 29, 31, 32
Cooper, Terry 78, 79
Coppell, Steve 65, 80, 81
Costacurta, Alessandro 17, 44, 56
Coventry City 31, 98
Croatia 33
Crompton, Bob 90
Cross, David 99
Cruyff, Johan 89
Cuba 89
Cunningham, Laurie 80
Czechoslovakia 51, 68, 74, 75, 78, 80, 81, 88, 89

D

Dalglish, Kenny 47, 49
Di Livio, Angelo 25, 44
Dean, Dixie 90
Del Piero, Alessandro 43
Denmark 72, 91
Derby County 90, 97
Devonshire, Alan 99
Di Matteo, Roberto *17*
Didi 73

Dienst, Gottfried 76
Dutch East Indies 89
Dynamo Tbilisi 13

E

East Germany 97
Ebwelle, Eugene 87
Edwards, Duncan 72
Egypt 86
England Members Club 32
Euro 96 8, 10, 16, 24, 29, 35, 39, 40, 51, 53, 55, 62
Eusebio 77, *77*, 95
Evans, Roy 52
Everton 9, 40, 90, 91, 101, 102

F

Ferdinand, Les 11, 12,*12*, 15, 24, 45
Ferdinand, Rio 45, *45*
Ferguson, Alex 9, 40
Ferrara, Ciro 57
FIFA 20, 29, 30, 67, 88, 89
FIFA rankings 8, 22, 30, 31, 36
Finney, Tom 68, 71, 73
Flowers, Ron 74, 75, *75*
Flowers, Tim 38, *38*
Fowler, Robbie 35, *35*, 45, 55, 57, 93
France 22, 29, 30, *31*, 33, 64, 67, 68, 75, 76, 77, 80, *80*, 81, 93, 100
Francis, Trevor 65, 80, 81
Fulham 74

G

Gaetjens, Joe 69
Galba, Karol 76
Garrincha 73
Gascoigne, Paul 10, *10*, 11, 14, 15, 16, 18, 20, 21, 24, 25, *26*, 27, 37, *37*, 39, 48, 49, 51, *51*,

53, 61, 63, 65, 86, 87, *89*, 103, *107*

Georgia 8, 12, 13, 14, 15, 18, *18*, 20, 22, 23, 47, 49, 55

Germany 8, 28, 30, 33, 55, *65*, 71, 72, 76, 77, 78–9, 81, 87, 88, 89, 92, 94, 95, 96, 97, 102, 104, *107*

Ghiggia 69

Golden Goal 35

Gorman, John 59

Grabowski, Jürgen 79

Greaves, Jimmy 74, 77, 92, 93, *93*, 96, 102

Green, Alan 53

Greenwood, Ron 60, 65, 71, 80, 81, *81*, 89, 97, 98, 99

Gullit, Ruud 86

H

Hagi, Gheorghe 31

Haller, Helmut 76, 77

Hamburg 98

Hardy, Sam 90

Hateley, Mark 82, 83

Haynes, Johnny 72, 74

Hinchcliffe, Andy 9, 10, 11, 12, 61

Hoddle, Glenn *4*, *7*, 8, 9, *9*, 11, 12, 13, 14, 15, 16, 17, 18, 20, 21–2, 23, 24, 25, *27*, 28, 29, 29, 31, 32, 33, 35, 36, 37, 39, 40, 41, 43, 44, 45, 46, 47, *47*, *47*, 48, 50, 51, 52, 53, 54, 55, 56, 57, 58–64, *58–64*, 65, 98

Hodge, Steve 83

Holland 39, 55, 86, 87, *88*, 89, 91

Horlock, Kevin 61

Houllier, Gerard 54

Howe, Don 73

Howells, David 44

Hughes, Emlyn 65, 89

Hungary 65, 67, 70, 71, 72, 73, 74, 77, 80, 89, 91, 99

Hunt, Roger 76, 77

Hunter, Norman 78, 79, 94

Hurst, Geoff 65, 76, 77, 78, *79*, 83, 93, 94, 96, 99, 102

I

Iceland 31

Ince, Paul 10, 11, 16, 18, 20, 21, *21*, 25, *26*, 29, 29, 37, 43, 47, 48, *48*, 49, 59, 61

Internazionale 18

Inzaghi, Filippo 25

Iordanescu, Anghel 31

Ipswich Town 64, 65, 80

Irwin, Dennis 41

Italy 8, 12, 13, 15, 16, *16*, 17, 18, 20, 22, 23, 24, 25, *25*, 26, 28, 29, 30, 33, 39, *39*, 41, 43, 44, 46, 47, 48, 50, 51, 54, *54*, 56, 57, 62, 67, 71, 74, *75*, 77, 81, 88, 89, 90, 97, 103, 104

J

Jacquet, Aimé 35

Jairzinho 78

Japan 40, *40*

Johns, Hugh 95

Juninho 42

Juventus 103

K

Keegan, Kevin 47, 49, 63, 80, 81, 89, 98, *98*, 99

Ketsbaia, Temur 18

Kevan, Derek *72*, 73

Kinkladze, Georgiou 13, 18, 20

Kipiani, David 18

Klinsmann, Jürgen 56

Koeman, Ronald 39

Kunde, Emmanuel 87

Kuwait 80

L

Lampard Sr., Frank 99

Lawton, Tommy 91, *91*

Le Saux, Graeme *7*, 16, 18, 20, 21, 24, 25, 33, 42, *42*, 43, 59, 61

Le Tissier, Matthew 10, 16, 17

Le Tournoi 22, 24, 29, *29*, 32, 33, 34, *34*, 35, 36, 38, 40, 41, 44, 46, 50, 52, 53, 54, *54*, 56, 57

Lee, Francis 78

Lee, Robert 18, 20, 21, *30*, 31, *34*, 49, *49*

Leeds United 39, 47, 89

Leicester City 57, 95, 97, 102

Lewin, Gary 48

Leyton Orient 97

Liechtenstein 31

Lineker, Gary 57, 65, 82, *82*, 83, *83*, 86, 87, 93, 101, 102, *102*, 103, *106*

Lithuania 31

Liverpool 52, 53, 90. 93, 97, 98, 99, 101

Lofthouse, Nat 70, 71, *71*, 72, 90

Luxembourg 74

Lyons, Chubby 69

M

Macedonia 31

Maier, Sepp 97

Maldini, Cesare 16, 23

Maldini, Paolo 25

Manchester City 13, 91

Manchester United 9, 37, 40, 41, 48, 50, 54, 56, 68, 72, 80, 81, 92, 100

Mannion, Wilf 68, 69

Manuel, Carlos 82

Maradona, Diego 82, 83, *83*

Mariner, Paul 80, 81

Martyn, Nigel 38

Massing, Benjamin 87

Matthews, Stanley 68, *68*, 69, 70, 72, 97

McIlvenney, Eddie 69

McMahon, Steve 86

McManaman, Steve 11, 16, 37, 52, *52*

McMenemy, Laurie 80

Merrick, Gil 71

Merson, Paul 38

Mexico 18, *35*, 76, 77

Middlesbrough 10, 42, 72, 100

Milan 93

Milburn, Jackie 69

Milla, Roger 87

Mills, Mick 80

Millwall 56

Moldova 8, 9, 10, *10*, 13, 22, *22*, 23, *23*, 38, 41, 50, 55, 56, 57, 59, 61

Moldovan, Viorel 31

Monaco 61

Moore, Bobby 45, 63, 65, *65*, 74, 75, 76, 78, *78*, 79, 94, *94*, 95, 96, 99, 100

Moore, Brian 22, 24

Morocco *67*, 82

Mortensen, Stan 68, 69

Mullen, Jimmy 69, 71

Müller, Gerd 79, 89

Mullery, Alan 78, 79

Munich 1860 94

Munich air disaster 72, 92

N

N'Kono, Thomas 87

Nagoya Grampus Eight 102

Neville brothers 41, 54

Neville, Gary 10, 11, 16, 18, 21, 24, 25, 34, 40, *40*, 41, 61

Neville, Phil 24, 40, 41, *41*

Newcastle United 47, 49, 52, 53, 55, 98

Newton, Keith 78

Nicholson, Bill 93

North Korea 77

Northern Ireland 68, 101

Norway 56

Norwich City 96

Nottingham Forest 56, 97

Notts County 91

Nowak, Piotr 11, 12

O

Owen, Michael 57

P

Pallister, Gary 61

Paraguay 31, 82, *82*, 102

Parker, Paul 87

Pearce, Stuart 11, 16, 17, 18, 42, 54, 61, 86, 87

Pele 34, 73, 77, 79, 95

Peru 94

Peruzzi, Angelo 25, 26

Peterborough United 39

Peters, Martin 65, 76, 77, 79, 94, 96, *96*, 99

Petrescu, Dan 31

Piechniczek, Antoni 11

Platini, Michel 23, 32

Platt, David 49, 65, 86, *86*, 87, 96, 103, *103*

Plymouth Argyle 97

Poland 8, 11, 12, 15, 20, 21, *21*, 39, 40, 41, 44, 46, 49, 55, 56, 57, 82, 83, *83*, 89, 94, 102

Portugal 67, 74, 77, *77*, 82, 91, 92, 95, 96

Preston North End 73, 94

PSV Eindhoven 65

Puskas, Ferenc 70

Q

QPR 39, 45

R

Rahn, Helmut 71

Ramsey, Sir Alf 22, 33, 63, 64, *64*, 67, 75, 76, 77, 78, 79, 89, 93, 94, 96, 104

Rangers 51

Rattin, Antonio 77
Redknapp, Harry 45, 53
Redknapp, Jamie 49, 53, *53*
Reid, Peter 83, 102
Republic of Ireland 31, 72, 86, 100
Revie, Don 64, 67, 89, 99
Rijkaard, Frank 45
Rix, Graham 80
Roberto Carlos 41
Robson, Bobby 31, 32, 33, 43, 51, *51*, 60, 62, 63, 65, *65*, *67*, 74, 80, 82, 83, *83*, 86, 87, 97, 98
Robson, Bryan 54, 65, 80, *80*, 81, 82, 83, 100, *100*
Romanenco, Denis 10
Romania 28, *28*, 29, 30, 31, *31*. 32, 49, 78
Ronaldo 33, 34, *34*
Rummenigge, Karlheinz 81
Rush, Ian 52

S

Sacchi, Arrigo 17
St John, Ian 93
Sampdoria 103
San Marino 101
Sansom, Kenny 82
Schiaffino, Juan Alberto 69
Schillaci, Salvatore 'Toto' 87
Scholes, Paul 22, 23, 24, 35, 54, *54*, 55, 57
Schumacher, Harald 81
Scifo, Enzo 87
Scotland 39, 40, 53, 55, 68, 70, 71, 88, 92, 93, 95, 96, 102
Scunthorpe United 98
Seaman, David 11, 16, 25, 36, 38, 39, *39*, 61
Seeler, Uwe 79
Sellimi, Adel 31
Shankly, Bill 98
Sharpe, Lee 38
Shearer, Alan 10, 11, *11*, 12, 13, *13*, 14, 16, *16*, 18, *18*, 20, 21, 23, 24, *31*, 35, 37, *37*, 39, 40, 42, 46, 48, 55, *55*, 57, 61
Sheedy, Kevin 86
Sheffield United 52
Sheringham, Teddy 15, 16, 18, 20, 21, 24, 25, 46, 56, *56*
Shilton, Peter 38, 81, 82, *83*, 86, 87, 92, 94, 97, *97*, *109*
Shreeves, Peter 60
Slater, Bill 73
Slimane, Mehdi 31

Smith, Walter 51
South Africa 20, 30, *30*, 44, 53, 57, *57*
Southampton 38, 55, 97, 98
Southgate, Gareth 10, 11, 21, 24, 25, *25*, 34, 45, 46, *46*, 61
Spain 30, 39, 67, 69, 81, 88, 98, 99
Steven, Trevor 83
Stevens, Gary 102
Stiles, Nobby 76, 77, *77*
Stoke City 68, 95, 97
Sunderland 91
Sweden 88, 89, 102
Swift, Frank 68, 91
Swindon Town 61
Switzerland 31, 53, 55, 71, 88

T

Taylor, Graham 38, 43, 47, 62, 65, *88*, 89, 101, 102, 103
Taylor, Peter 59
Taylor, Tommy 72
Thompson, Phil 80
Tichy, Lajos 74
Tie breaks 35
Tottenham Hotspur 44, 56, 60, 61, 90, 93, 96, 102
Tunisia 28, *28*, 29, 30, 31, 32

U

Umbro Cup 38, 40, 49
United States 31, 69
Uruguay 67, 69, 70, 71, *71*, 76, 77, 88–9
USSR 47, 60, 72, 73, 77

V

Valderrama, Carlos 31
Van Basten, Marco 86
Van Breukelen, Hans 87
Vava 73
Venables, Terry 8, 9, 10, 24, 41, 43, 45, 47, 49, 58, 59, 62, 64, 100, 103
Vieri, Christian 26, 39

W

Waddle, Chris 51, 83, 86, 87, 98
Wales 68, 73, 88, 98
Walker, Des 86
Walker, Ian 16, 17, 38
Walsh, Steve 57

Watford 101
Weber, Wolfgang 76, 77
Wenger, Arsène 43, 61
West Bromwich Albion 100
West Germany *see* Germany
West Ham United 45, *45*, 65, 94, 96, 99
Wilkins, Ray *67*, 80, 81, 82, 83
Wilkinson, Howard 47, 62
Wilshaw, Denis 71
Wilson, Bob 39
Wilson, Ray 76
Wimbledon 9, 50
Winterbottom, Walter 64, 68, 72, 73, 74, *74*, 75, 91
Wolstenholme, Kenneth 92
Wolverhampton Wanderers 73, 75
Woodcock, Tony 102
Woodward, Vivian 90, 92,
World Cup 1930 88–9
World Cup 1934 89
World Cup 1938 89
World Cup 1950 67, 68–9, *68*, 69, 91, 104
World Cup 1954 70–71, *70*, *71*, 104
World Cup 1958 72–3, *72*, *73*, 104
World Cup 1962 74–5, 92, 93, 104
World Cup 1966 28, 64, *66*, 67, 76–7, *76*, 77, 92, 93, 94, 95, *96*, *104*

World Cup 1970 28, 64, 789, *78*, *79*, 92, 95, 104
World Cup 1974 89, 98
World Cup 1978 89, 98
World Cup 1982 28, 65, 67, 80–81, *80*, 97, 98, 99, 104
World Cup 1986 28, 65, 67, *67*, 82–3, *82*, *83*, 97, 100, 101, 102
World Cup 1990 28, 51, 65, 86–7, *86*, *87*, 97, 102, 103, *103*, *107*
World Cup 1994 9, *88*, 89, *89*, 103, 1994 104
Wozniak, Andrzej 112 12, 21
Wright, Billy 68, 69, *69*, 70, 71, 73, *73*, 75, 94, 100
Wright, Ian *5*, *23*, 24, 25, 26, *36*, 43, 54, 57, *57*, 63
Wright, Mark 86, 87
Wright, Tommy 78

Y

Yashin, Lev 72
Yugoslavia 71, 87, 88, 96

Z

Zagallo, Mario 75
Zico 60
Zola, Gianfranco 17, 44, 46

Acknowledgements

The publishers would like to thank the following sources for their kind permission to reproduce the pictures in this book:

Action Images 4,6,31t; **Allsport** 16,32,36, 55, 60, 63, 64, 65, 67, 74, 80, 81, 83, 84/85, 86, 94, 97, 99/ **Shaun Botterill** 9, 21, 24, 30t, 34t, 35, 38, 39, 41, 44, 48, 54, 56, 89; **Clive Brunskill** 14, 15, 19, 22, 23, 40, 43, 47, 49, 50, 53, 103; **David Cannon** 82,100,107,109; Chris Cole 88; Michael Cooper 30b; **Stu Forster** 17,37; Hulton Getty 66, 68, 69, 70, 71, 72, 73, 75, 76, 77, 78, 79, 90, 91, 92, 93, 95, 96, 104; **Michael King** 106; **Ross Kinnaird** 5, 12, 13, 18, 26, 27, 51, 58, 59; **Steve Powell** 98; **Gary Prior** 101; **Ben Radford** 10, 11, 22, 25, 31b, 34b, 46, 57, 61, 62, 102; **Dan Smith** 45, 52; **Billy Stickland** 87; **Vandystadt** 28, 29, 33, 42

Every effort has been made to acknowledge correctly and contact the source and/or copyright holder of each picture, and Carlton Books Limited apologises for any unintentional errors or omissions which will be corrected in future editions of this book.